The Secret Powers Of Colorful Foods

Enhancing trust, sensuality, self-confidence,
love, forgiveness, intuition and spirituality

by

Patricia Dennis and Charlotte Lyons

BALBOA.
PRESS
A DIVISION OF HAY HOUSE

Cover and text design by Dennis Hodgson
www.dhodgsonart.com

Balboa Press books may be ordered through booksellers or by contacting:

Balboa Press
A Division of Hay House
1663 Liberty Drive
Bloomington, IN 47403
www.balboapress.com
1 (877) 407-4847

Because of the dynamic nature of the Internet, any web addresses or links contained in this book may have changed since publication and may no longer be valid. The views expressed in this work are solely those of the author and do not necessarily reflect the views of the publisher, and the publisher hereby disclaims any responsibility for them.

The authors of this book, Patricia Dennis and Charlotte Lyons, have provided information and techniques to help you achieve clearing and balancing of the chakra system. They are not dispensing medical or psychological advice; this informational guide is not meant to treat, diagnose or prescribe. Always consult a qualified physician or appropriate health care professional for any medical, psychological or physical conditions or symptoms. Neither author accepts any responsibility for your health or how you choose to use the information contained in this book.

Stock photography and illustrations from dreamstime.com

ISBN: 978-1-4525-8605-2 (sc)
ISBN: 978-1-4525-8606-9 (e)

Library of Congress Control Number: 2013920245

Printed in the United States of America.

Balboa Press rev. date: 01/14/2014

Acknowledgments

A heartfelt "Thank you!" goes to...

Jari Smith for her guidance and encouragement every step of the way.
Anne Raymond and Reenah McGill for their inspiration.
Dennis Hodgson for his art direction and design.
My husband and soul mate, Emmett Brown, for his love and support.

And with utmost gratitude, I thank my other angels, my spirit guides, that
have brought me this far...

-P.D.

My sincere thanks to all my family and friends for their support, inspiration

and encouragement during the creation of this book. Special thanks to my son

Chris and my Mother for their patience and understanding.

-C.L.

CONTENTS

Authors' Note

How many of us can say we get enough fruits and vegetables into our diet every day? Selecting them can seem humdrum for some. For others who are not "foodies" or vegans per se, it can be considered nothing more than a nutritional obligation.

What if you knew there is a hidden exchange of information between the energy of food's colors and our mental, emotional and spiritual states? What if you knew the color of a certain fruit or vegetable could be a color of a feeling, a sense, a mental state of mind, even an emotion that affects your everyday life? What if you went to the fruit and vegetable section of the market with a particular challenge in mind, knowing a color of a fruit or vegetable could possibly help you with it? Wouldn't you look at those magnificent rainbow colors differently?

In addition to pleasing our taste buds and supplying nutrients to the physical body, fruits and vegetables can affect feelings, attitudes, thoughts and emotions. Knowing that can make shopping and eating fruits and vegetables far more interesting – even fun. It is our hope that *The Secret Powers Of Colorful Foods* intrigues and enlightens you so that you consciously choose foods in a more life-enhancing way.

- Patricia Dennis and Charlotte Lyons

Introduction

It seems like life in this high speed technological era is deluged with new advancements every second. This bombardment puts us into a hypnotic state of addiction to cyberspace where we find connections with others but not ourselves. The more we partake of advances in cyberspace the more we need to become aware of feeding our "inner space" – the energy that powers our mind, feelings and spirit.

We are more aware than ever of healthier eating habits and an appreciation of food's nutritional value. We are learning that foods of the earth - fruits, vegetables, spices and herbs, or rainbow foods - are our real medicine chest. What many people don't know is that the outer colors of fruits and vegetables can help power our "inner space" physically invisible to the human eye.

Secrets That Can Benefit Everyone

You will discover how chakras or energy centers in your body feed off the vibrations or energetic frequencies from color pigments in rainbow foods. The book reveals that feelings, judgments and spiritual acceptance are also driven by color. When you apply what you have learned from *The Secret Powers Of Colorful Foods* you will select fruits and vegetables with a fresh eye and a different purpose.

In our research we found varied perspectives on the topic of food, mood and chakras. We have studied different interpretations and present them to you from our viewpoint. In doing so, we have simplified the chakra system to make it more understandable. We have taken colors of the chakras and assigned them to corresponding thoughts and emotions, making it simpler to match a rainbow food to an emotion. To make it more interesting, you will find visualizations, exercises, interesting facts about food and party tips.

How To Use This Book

PART I shows you how to select colorful foods according to your mental, emotional and spiritual needs. You'll notice we do not dwell on the relationship of rainbow foods and the physical body. We do not venture into the specifics of physical health; rather, we present ways rainbow foods can affect one's mental state, emotions and stirrings of the soul.

PART II offers foods and recipes for seven chakras (the seventh chakra only discusses breath work and meditation as that is what it feeds on.) You will also find affirmations and exercises to help balance each color.

PART III serves up everything you have learned so that you can have a real party with colorful foods. Our Rainbow Broth recipe is filled with delicious nutrients from the colors. You will learn to customize it your specific color or colors using purée shortcuts. Plus, you'll learn how to host a *Rainbow Foods Party* with tasty appetizers, *Rainbow Shooters* and a card game.

We suggest you first read PART I, *Seeing The Value Of Color In Foods For The First Time*, to familiarize yourself with making food choices. When you determine which color you would like to use first, go directly to PART II, *Foods And Recipes By Color*. It gives more detailed information on the balancing power of each rainbow color. You can select from deliciously simple recipes created by Charlotte Lyons, cookbook author, food editor and culinary consultant.

While flipping to the first color you select is key to your immediate interest, it's important to learn about each of the other colors too. Each color contributes to mental, emotional and spiritual well-being in different ways. The energies of colors build upon each other, advancing knowledge and emotional development from one chakra to the next. And, different colors are affected in different environments, so your needs may change. After becoming comfortably familiar with PART I and PART II, go to PART III - *Playing With Rainbow Foods*.

Affirmations And Exercises

Throughout the book, you will find meditations, affirmations and exercises that help to liberate blocked energy centers. When you are mindful of a challenge you are experiencing and put to use *The Secret Powers Of Colorful Foods*, you are feeding your subconscious mind with tools of change. To enhance support of your energy centers, we recommend you do the exercises for each food color – before you begin to prepare the recipes. Keep the affirmation or positive statement in mind as you prepare and consume the food. Being an active participant in your own energy balancing offers greater rewards.

"It's the repetition of affirmations that leads to belief.
And once that belief becomes deep conviction,
things begin to happen."

- Claude M. Bristol

"*The day is coming when a single carrot,
freshly observed,
will set off a revolution.*"

- Paul Cezanne

PART I

SEEING THE VALUE OF COLOR IN FOODS FOR THE FIRST TIME

Most of us know that foods grown in earth's soil offer vitamins and minerals that nourish our physical bodies. But did you know it is the color pigments in rainbow foods that provide an energy supply that helps support and balance our emotional feelings and spirit?

When you shop for fruits and vegetables, what do you really see? An ingredient for a meal? An attractive taste? Chances are, you see a lemon, not the yellow color. If you did view it for its sunny vibration, you might think, *I've got a meeting coming up; I can use something yellow to support my confidence and intellect.* You might look at asparagus and see a bunch of the spears in a rubber band. If you focused on the rich green color, you might say to yourself, *I can use these to help release resentment and heal my broken heart.*

Colorful Foods Have Particular Health Benefits For The Body

News reports linking the bio-chemicals in the pigments of fruits and vegetables to health are coming out daily. Doctors and nutritionists emphasize guidelines for consuming them. In fact, it is recommended that we have a minimum of two and a half cups of vegetables a day to help us thrive. While the importance of eating colorful fruits and vegetables (or rainbow eating) for our physical health is at the forefront of the news, that is only half of the story – the biological part. The other half of the story is how colorful fruits, vegetables and herbs also nourish soul consciousness – the psychological, emotional aspects of ourselves. We are aware that brightly colored vegetables contain disease fighting phyto-chemicals. It is the color pigments that are the heroes.

The website, *Squidoo,* has fascinating articles, one titled, "The Art of Eating in Living Color," and another – "Colorful Creative Cooking." It is from the latter article, that we selected the following quote:

"...Analysis of pigments reveals that colorful fruit and vegetables are not just visually appetizing, but positively good for you because each color is related to a different phyto-chemical that has particular health benefits. It is the color pigments that are the real super nutrients and these are as important to our health as vitamins and minerals."

Each Color Can Also Affect Psychological And Spiritual Well-Being

How can that be? Well, we have to see ourselves as having two bodies. One is physical, that you can experience with the senses. The other is what we call metaphysical: invisible to the human eye. We feed our physical body with foods. We feed our non-physical body with subtle energies - vibrations given off by colors in foods, sound, even thoughts.

Just as our physical body has bones, muscles, nerves, and cells, our non-physical body is a network of energy centers that power all of our bodily functions. The major energy centers are located along the spinal column, from its base up through the top of the skull. Each energy center has its own color frequency. When we consume a food of a similar color or frequency, we feed that energy center. When we know which colored food feeds which energy center, we can heighten psychological and spiritual energy. As you feed your energy centers, you feed your soul.

Where This Idea Came From

According to ancient Hindu Vedic texts created thousands of years ago, it was believed that along the spine, neck and skull of the body were spinning, disc shaped energy centers. In Sanskrit, they were known as "chakras," pronounced chak-ruhz. These electrical forces moved in a clockwise direction at different speeds. The seven major chakras emitted seven colors: red, orange, yellow, green, aquamarine, purple and violet.

When the chakras are clear and clean of debris caused by stress, fear and anger, and are properly aligned, our inner life is balanced. On the other hand, when there is emotional trauma, it creates a blockage – clogged chakras can become sluggish and out of balance, which leads to physical and mental distress. As energy spirals from one chakra to another, like a pulley system, one chakra that's slowed down or weak or out of balance can make all chakras imbalanced.

De-Mystifying The Mysterious Chakras

Since 2500 B.C., East Indian and Chinese healing systems have utilized chakras in their treatments. While mainstream Western medicine does not use the chakra system, Western culture is becoming more aware of it. There are medical and scientific communities that acknowledge the importance of the chakras and feeding them with energy. Skeptics might have an attitude change when they hear what experts have to say.

Modern Science Catches Up With Ancient Philosophy

Dr. Oz, for example, is a big proponent of the chakras. Just look at the article "Balancing The Chakras Through Food" on his website:

"The energy of light has an intimate connection with our bodies. As the sun's rays fall onto the earth, these vibrations are expressed through the color of the plant, vegetable, or flower – each color holds an energy that nourishes the individual chakras. Eating a variety of colors with each meal is important in keeping the chakras balanced through food."

On his blog, Jonathan Parker states:

"The chakras are subtle energy centers that act as doorways through which emotional, mental, and spiritual forces flow in and out of our bodies. They are openings through which our attitudes, beliefs, and emotions are processed and stored. Another way to think of the chakras is they are somewhat like little computers which have unique ways of processing and storing our mental and emotional experiences."

The website *finerminds.com* tells us:

"Chakras are collecting pools of subtle energy and subtle energy is by nature very sensitive to mental, emotional, physical and spiritual inputs."

According to Dr. Mark Hyman's Gaiam blog:

"Food contains information that speaks to our genes, not just calories for energy. We are learning from research in the field of nutrigenomics that food 'talks' to our DNA, switching on or off genes that lead to health or disease. What you eat programs your body with messages of health or illness."

When interviewed about the chakras, Dr. Candace Pert, American neuroscientist, pharmacologist and author of the book *Molecules of Emotion* had this to say:

"I've been lecturing about the chakras for many years. It's so fascinating how this ancient wisdom corresponds to modern science - I was shocked. My chakras were shocked! I realized in 1987 that areas along the axis, from the top of the forehead to the base of the spine, these classical chakras areas corresponded to what I called 'nodal points' - places where lots of neurotransmitters and neuropeptides were released."

Thinking along similar lines, one of the foremost authorities on chakras, Dr. Anodea Judith asserts:

"Chakras refer to a spinning sphere of bio-energetic activity emanating from the major nerve ganglia branching forward from the spinal column."

Another foremost authority, and internationally-known nutritionist, Dr. Deanna Minich, describes the energetic connection between food and the chakras:

"Food particles carry a specific vibration. The vibration feeds the chakras; chakras become activated."

How Do You Know Which Chakras Are Out Of Balance?

When we are out of balance emotionally and spiritually, we know. We can recognize a particular area that is bothering us or observe it in those we care about. Our mind speaks to us in metaphors that we can use to connect to a chakra responsible for an emotion. For example, you may feel stuck in your life and can't make a move. Or you may feel the opposite, uprooted in some way. Or think, *you don't have a leg to stand on*. You will discover in later reading, that the root chakra, lowest on the spine and closest to the ground, relates to our moving forward in life. Maybe a loss or disappointment has left you downhearted or heart broken. Those words speak to emotions in the area of the upper chest. Then again, you might be yellow bellied and have a courage deficiency in your power chakra in the waist area.

When you recognize which emotion or thwarted intention bothers you the most, you can work on balancing it by feeding the chakra food of a corresponding colored food. Remember, when the electrical energy of the chakras is exposed to the biochemical energies of color pigment, it can clear clogged chakras so that they are open to the energy flow of life.

What Causes Chakras To Be Blocked?

Usually blockage comes from energy interference - some kind of trauma at an early age. It could be from defense mechanisms we developed as children that have been "hard wired" into the chakra system that our subconscious mind has become familiar and comfortable with. It could be we developed emotional numbness to cope with trauma. It could be the accumulation of negative electrical charges that come from negative and fearful thoughts.

How we react to situations has a great deal to do with depletion of our energies. If we think the worst, if we imagine terrible things, the thought alone can knock a chakra out of balance. That's why it is a good practice to immediately switch to a positive thought as soon as you observe yourself thinking otherwise. Observe the negative words in your speech and reframe them. In the Aquamarine section of this book, we suggest ways for you to do that.

Other ways to overcome imbalances in the chakra system include meditation, deep breathing, visual imagery, healing sounds, aromatherapy and body movement.

How Emotions Affect The Chakras

Behind every thought there is an energy vibration.
The vibration of negative thoughts can disrupt the chakra system.

There is a wonderfully informative book written by Dr. Anodea Judith called *Eastern Body, Western Mind: Psychology And The Chakra System As A Path To The Self.* It tells us that there are emotions and states of mind that can disable chakras – just as negative emotions and thoughts weaken us physically and mentally. In her book, Dr. Anodea Judith refers to them as demons that affect *what she calls* "rights" that are associated with the chakras. Let's take a look at how those emotional "demons" take away our "rights."

1. *Root Chakra (Red)*
   Fear takes away...The right to be here

2. *Sacral Chakra (Orange)*
   Guilt takes away...The right to feel

3. *Navel Chakra (Yellow)*
   Shame takes away...The right to act

4. *Heart Chakra (Green)*
   Sorrow takes away...The right love and be loved

5. *Throat Chakra (Aquamarine)*
   Lies take away...The right to speak the truth

6. *Third Eye or Brow Chakra (Purple)*
   Illusion takes away...The right to see

7. *Crown Chakra (White, Gold, Violet)*
   Attachment takes away...The right to know

Chakra Colors Vibrate From Warm To Cool

The Root Chakra, red, is a hot/warm color that has to do with survival and feeling secure. It has everything to do with living in the physical, material world. The Sacral Chakra is a warm color, orange, that supports reproduction and creativity. The Solar Plexus Chakra, yellow, supports our ego, self-image, intellect and courage. *The first three energy centers: Red, Orange, and Yellow vibrate to warm colors which are stimulating.*

The Heart Chakra, green, cools the heat of the lower chakras with love. The Throat Chakra connects our lower energies of survival and ego to the more spiritual upper energies. Aquamarine vibrates to the frequency of liquid allowing one's voice to be heard. The Third Eye or Brow Chakra, purple, has the second slowest spin (Crown Chakra is slowest) allowing us to cool down through spirituality and meditation. *The second three energy centers: Green, Aquamarine, and Purple vibrate to cool colors which are relaxing.*

This is good to know, because if you are out of balance with too much of the warm colors, go to cool colors. If you are overstimulated by cool colors, you can select warm colors. For example, if you are a total right brained creative person, you can get spacey. To balance the cool color energy, you would need to be rooted in reality and select a red color – perhaps apples, beets or pomegranates to ground you. A yellow squash could also balance you with some left brained guidance. If you have overactive green and are ultra kind and giving without being loved in return, you might balance it with red or yellow. This is called chakra balancing which we do not explore in depth in this book. We are concentrating on the underactive chakras so that you can easily select one color. We do describe what an overactive and underactive chakra looks like so that you can see the difference.

Any Shade Of Color Works

In Paula Shaw's book, *Chakras*: *The Magnificent Seven Energy Centers For Healing*, she describes why we can use any shade of any color:

"Like sound, color vibrates at a very specific frequency, which determines the color you see. Every chakra has a predominant color that corresponds to its vibrational frequency."

According to Donna Eden, author of *Energy Medicine*, a chakra is rarely just one color.

"The seven layers of each chakra can vary in color according to what is going on energetically within that chakra."

Selecting The Color Of Food You Are Lacking

Very often, several or all chakras can be out of balance – remember, all it takes is one to throw off the other six. It is optimal to have all the rainbow colors in your daily diet. You could start with a rainbow salad or a soup, like the Rainbow Broth in Part III. Our simple, easy to prepare recipes in Part II of this book add to the enjoyment of empowering yourself with the knowledge of rainbow foods. Remember that our energies are always changing. Different life situations create different challenges for us. That's why it is good to familiarize yourself with all the colors so that you are prepared to bolster any of the underactive energies of the chakras.

On the following pages are charts that put emotional energies into color categories that correspond to the colors of foods.

Select A Mental Or Emotional Need	Select Color Of That Energy	Select Food That Is A Similar Color	Select Food That Is A Similar Color	Select Food That Is A Similar Color
Trusting Intuition **Insight** **Finding Your Purpose** **Integrity**	Purple			
Expressing True Feelings **Being Honest With Yourself**	Aquamarine *Liquids, Any Color*			
Nurturing **Love of Self & Others** **Forgiveness** **Compassion**	Green			
Having Self-Worth **Mental Clarity** **Courage To Do New Things**	Yellow			
Creative Expression **Sensuality/Sexuality** **Appetite For Life** **In Touch With Emotions**	Orange			
Grounded **Secure in Everyday Survival** **Sense of Belonging**	Red or Root Veggies			

Your Emotions Can Tell You Which Food Color You Need

Each of our energy centers can become imbalanced at any time. By observing your thoughts and behaviors, you can determine the food color you may need.

You May Need A Red Energy Boost If You Feel:

"I wish I had more energy to succeed."
"I worry about being ripped off."
"I am always late for everything."
"I feel insecure about what is happening next."
"I am spacey."
"I wish I were more practical or down to earth."
"I keep questioning my decisions."
"I feel invisible."
"I am alone and I can't connect with people."

You May Need An Orange Energy Boost If You Feel:

"I can't commit to romantic relationships. I just move on to the next."
"I know I am creative. I can't seem to do anything with it."
"I wish I weren't so stiff and uptight around people."
"I need more passion in my life."
"I wish I were free to dance and move my hips. But I am too self-conscious."
"I don't feel any joy in life."
"I would like to be able to have fun and go with the flow."
"I am afraid of enjoying my own sexuality."
"I am worthless because I have nothing to show for my life."

You May Need A Yellow Energy Boost If You Feel:

"I worry about what other people think."

"I have to keep proving myself."

"I don't stand up for myself."

"It's hard to make decisions when you think everyone else's is right."

"It seems so easy for others get ahead in life. What value do I have?"

"I wish I could have more self-respect."

"I want to be able to take on new challenges without fear."

"I cannot trust myself to totally take care of me."

"I wish I can manifest my deepest desires and reach my goals."

You May Need A Green Energy Boost If You Feel:

"My heart is heavy with resentment."

"I hate myself for what I did."

"I can't forgive others."

"I want to stop feeling sorry for myself."

"I just can't get over my broken heart."

"I don't deserve to be happy."

"I'm not worthy of love."

"I am always afraid of getting hurt. I wish I can feel peace."

"Who can love me if I can't love me?"

You May Need An Aquamarine Energy Boost If You Feel:

"I'm afraid of speaking my truth."

"I'd rather hope people do what I want rather than tell them truthfully."

"I say things to pacify others to avoid conflict."

"I only say things to make others happy."

"I hold back from being the best I can be."

"I wish I weren't so timid."

"Being around certain people, I get tongue-tied."

You May Need A Purple Energy Boost If You Feel:

"I sometimes feel like my emotions and thoughts are in conflict with each other."

"I don't feel like I have a life purpose."

"It's hard to make decisions quickly."

"I get depressed easily."

"How do I go beyond materialism to be more spiritual?"

"How can I trust my hunches more?"

"I wish I had more insight into situations."

Our Energy Centers And The Foods That Feed Them

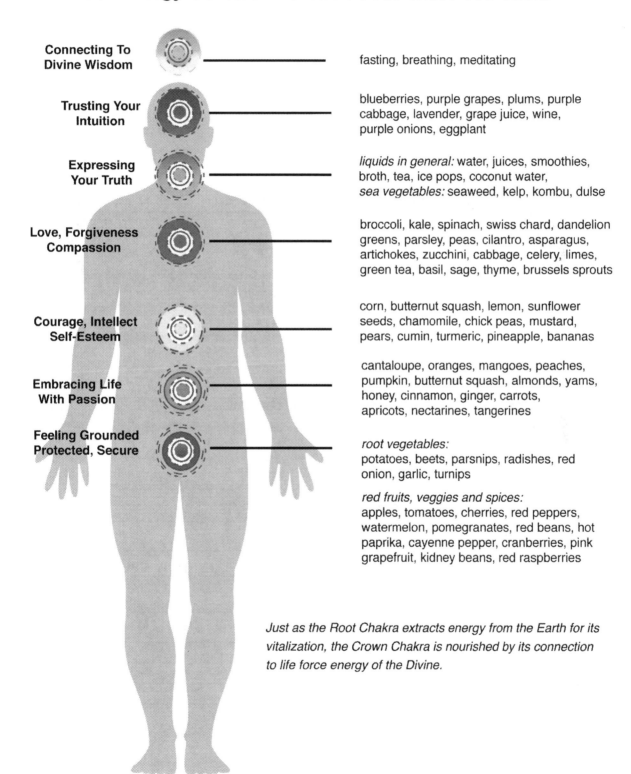

Connecting To Divine Wisdom — fasting, breathing, meditating

Trusting Your Intuition — blueberries, purple grapes, plums, purple cabbage, lavender, grape juice, wine, purple onions, eggplant

Expressing Your Truth — *liquids in general:* water, juices, smoothies, broth, tea, ice pops, coconut water, *sea vegetables:* seaweed, kelp, kombu, dulse

Love, Forgiveness Compassion — broccoli, kale, spinach, swiss chard, dandelion greens, parsley, peas, cilantro, asparagus, artichokes, zucchini, cabbage, celery, limes, green tea, basil, sage, thyme, brussels sprouts

Courage, Intellect Self-Esteem — corn, butternut squash, lemon, sunflower seeds, chamomile, chick peas, mustard, pears, cumin, turmeric, pineapple, bananas

Embracing Life With Passion — cantaloupe, oranges, mangoes, peaches, pumpkin, butternut squash, almonds, yams, honey, cinnamon, ginger, carrots, apricots, nectarines, tangerines

Feeling Grounded Protected, Secure — *root vegetables:* potatoes, beets, parsnips, radishes, red onion, garlic, turnips

red fruits, veggies and spices: apples, tomatoes, cherries, red peppers, watermelon, pomegranates, red beans, hot paprika, cayenne pepper, cranberries, pink grapefruit, kidney beans, red raspberries

Just as the Root Chakra extracts energy from the Earth for its vitalization, the Crown Chakra is nourished by its connection to life force energy of the Divine.

Chakra Cleansing Exercises

Just as you brush your teeth every day, it's a good idea to clean your chakras of any negative energy residues. Here are a couple of simple exercises to do morning and night. Select a private spot without distractions to do the following exercises.

The Daily Tune Up

Focus on your breath. Visualize, picture or imagine your seven energy centers. Make sure each chakra is spinning clockwise. If they aren't, with your fingers, gently tap the particular chakra on your physical body, then move your forefinger around in a clockwise direction. You can use your mental energy to reverse the spin by imagining the chakra spinning clockwise if it is spinning counter clockwise.

You can also use your forefinger to make a circle in the air near the chakra so it rotates in the right direction and fast enough. The seventh chakra, violet, spins the slowest, and each chakra spins a little faster than the last. With practice, you'll find that energy of the chakras and their colors speak to you wordlessly.

White Light Cleanse

- Visualize or imagine a violet white halo circling over the crown of your head. It is spinning clockwise.

- Now imagine the purple chakra above the eyebrows in the middle of the head spinning clockwise.

- Proceed to the aquamarine throat chakra. Then the green heart chakra. The yellow chakra. The orange chakra. The red chakra.

- Let any energy that doesn't serve you be released down the legs, through the toes into the Earth.

- Now imagine that you are facing your body and see the colorful rainbow energies all lit up spinning properly in perfect balance.

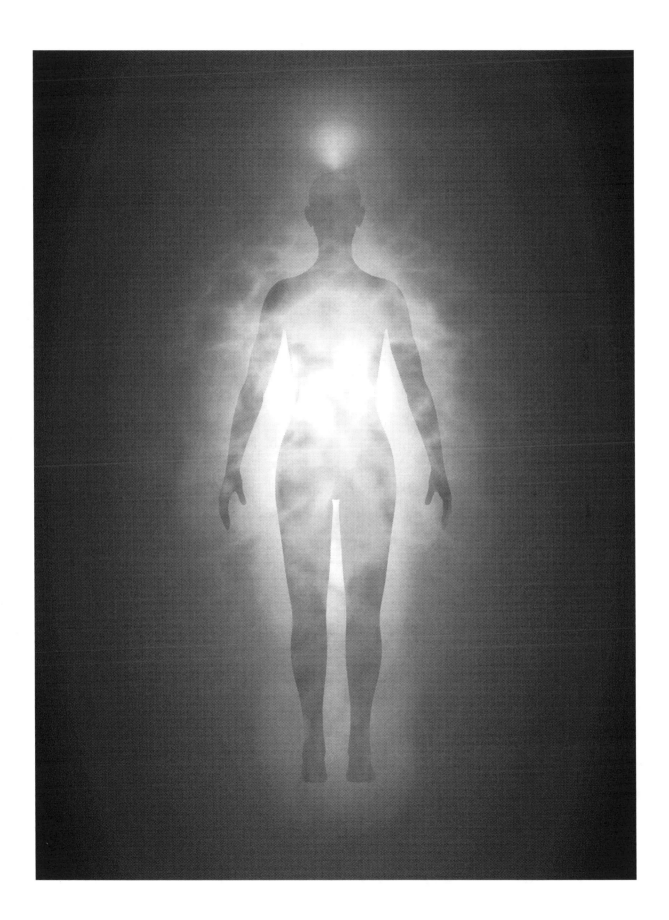

Questions And Answers

Q: If you can't see chakras or the energy centers, how do we know they really exist?

A: You can't see wind, but you can see its effects. You can't see gravity, but you know it's there. Chakra energy drives the organs, muscles, and cells of our physical body in addition to affecting our mental, emotional and spiritual well-being.

Q: Where does chakra energy come from?

A: A physical explanation could be that along the spine are a series of nerves that emit electrical charges. These charges supply energy to the chakras.

Q: Once I figure out the color I need, how often do I need to consume the food that corresponds to that color?

A: Hypnotherapists advise clients that it takes at least 21 days of repetition to create a new habit that the subconscious mind will accept. If you have a particular issue that is ongoing, we recommend having vegetables whose color corresponds to that emotion. We suggest you do not eat the same exact vegetable the same way each day. Use moderation, but have that color in your diet along with other colors. Interact with your inner self as to the portion size.

Q: How do I know if a chakra is becoming strengthened?

A: Changes take form as subtle energies. Being conscious of what you are eating and knowledge of the power of color helps feed the subconscious mind. You will get a sense that there is change.

Q: If I need more than one color, what do I do?

A: You can use different colors in a broth, salad or smoothie. Roast veggies. Or enjoy raw food snacks like carrots and celery with almond butter. Be creative!

Q: If the chakras power the body and the mind, what powers the chakras?

A: Breath, water, rainbow colors, aromas, tastes, touch, sound – the senses.

A Quickie Review

Chakras are energy centers that extend from the base of the spine to the top of the head. They spin clockwise creating a force that supports your physical health and your psychological and spiritual well-being. Each chakra is associated with a particular color and different emotion, mental state and physical part of the body. To function at an optimum level, all chakras must be open, allowing energy to flow, supplying you with more energy and balance in life. When one of the chakras becomes clogged and weakened by emotional or physical stress, it slows down and becomes unbalanced so that it can't transfer energy properly to the other chakras. That's why it is important to keep all of your chakras tuned up and in complete balance.

- Anatomically, the chakras correspond to nerve centers in the body and they are physically fueled by the senses including color and aroma and sound. They are also empowered by thought, breath and meditation.

- Our chakras are responsible for the energy flow from one part of the body to another and are associated with our physical, mental, emotional and spiritual states.

- Through stress of any kind, physical, emotional or psychological, our chakras can become unbalanced or out of tune. They can be come underactive or overactive.

- When energy does not flow freely from the chakras, the body does not function properly - we become mentally, emotionally and spiritually out of whack. We need to re-establish the free flow of energy in order to heal.

- We can recharge the chakra or chakras that are weak by feeding the body foods whose colors correspond to the colors of the chakras and build spiritual muscle through visualizations.

QUIZ

1. Your friend tells you her grown son, formerly married to a pushy woman, is now dating another woman who also stifles him. What food colors would be the ingredients she could make in a dish for her son to be more expressive?

2. You meet a person who is very into spiritual things. So much so, he thinks everything that he does is really an act of the Divine and he takes no personal responsibility. What color would you suggest and what dish would you make?

3. You have to give a speech tomorrow. You are nervous and tongue tied when you practice. What would you prepare for dinner the night before?

4. You say you can never forgive your ex. What veggies would you have?

5. Oh, those dark days when everything seems bleak. What food color will perk you up and what would you prepare?

6. You have been procrastinating on a project. You must get moving on it. What colors will motivate you to do so?

7. You're a great multi-tasker and perfectionist. Thing is, you are now working overtime on everything. What color do you need to balance you out?

8. You have a sixth sense, you just don't trust it enough. What foods would you have to balance that energy?

9. You are in the supermarket. The person in line ahead of you has a basket filled with yellow zucchini, corn and bananas. What feeling is out of balance?

10. You don't like confrontations. In fact, you want everyone to love you. You tell people only what they want to hear, not what you want to say. What do you do to change?

ANSWERS

1. Yellow for logic, courage and setting boundaries. Aquamarine, a flavored water, to speak his truth openly and freely. Red to be grounded so he can stand up for himself.

2. Red for being down to earth and grounding in reality. Pomegranate Ginger Ale, and beet salad or any dish in the Red Section.

3. Something yellow for logic and aquamarine to lubricate the throat so that one's voice can be heard.

4. Green is the energy of forgiveness. Broccoli, spinach, purple kale, mint tea.

5. Anything yellow is sunshine on a cloudy day. Banana smoothie with flax seeds.

6. Orange is passion for creativity. Have orange juice or toast with honey and cinnamon.

7. Multi-taskers have overactive yellow energy. The mind has to be put into a calm, meditative state. Breathing, meditation and water intake help. Also a little purple: Red grapes, wine, blueberries, and other foods from the purple section.

8. To balance an underactive Brow Chakra, snack on purple grapes or figs.

9. An underactive yellow energy indicates lack of ego strength and depression. One needs more yellow to balance out confidence and courage.

10. You would increase your liquids, mainly water. You could flavor the water with lemon or cucumber. Or have a fruit ice pop! The recipe is in the Aquamarine section.

"The soul becomes dyed with the color of its thoughts."

- Marcus Aurelius

PART II

FOODS AND RECIPES BY COLOR

Now that you have selected a color to work with, it's good to clarify exceptions to the rule. The Root Chakra (red) also includes the colors brown and black, giving mushrooms their earthy place. Garlic, potatoes and white onions are included too because they are root vegetables.

Another point is, the color green appears to have more shades than any other color. That's because it has warm (yellow) and cool (blue) in it. So there is jade green to pea green, to leaf green to olive and celery. For the purposes of this book, all shades of green will fall into the green chakra category. Cauliflower, which appears white, is in the broccoli family and will also be included in the Green section.

In the Aquamarine section - the focus is on water or the sea. We offer suggestions for ways to give water taste appeal, including lemon, cucumber or mint water, ice cubes frozen with a fruit mixture and smoothies of all colors. The common factor is liquid or water; it is not so much dependant on how the ultimate color comes out.

Rainbow Foods Shortcuts

Naturally, it is best to use fresh fruits and veggies when we prepare a recipe. However, there are many convenient substitutions – canned, bottled, bagged, jarred or frozen foods - that work very nicely.

RED: Canned or bottled tomato juice and mixed vegetable juice; canned tomatoes, tomato paste, tomato sauce, pasta sauce, prepared tomato soup; prepared tomato salsa; pre-sliced pink grapefruit; watermelon in season.

RED/PURPLE: Bottled grape juice (100% juice), bottled cranberry juice or frozen cranberry juice concentrate, frozen whole berries, purple cabbage, frozen sliced red peppers and fresh apples, pears, berries and cherries.

ORANGE: Pre-washed and cut or shredded carrots, frozen carrots and frozen winter squash; pre-sliced mango available fresh-chilled or packed in juice or as frozen mango chunks; pre-cut cantaloupe wedges or balls; and whole fresh apricots.

ORANGE/YELLOW: Fresh orange juice, frozen orange juice or tangerine juice concentrate; pre-sliced papaya, pineapple, and yellow grapefruit sections available fresh or chilled and packed in juice; frozen pineapple chunks; pineapple canned in pineapple juice; fresh whole nectarines, oranges, peaches, and tangerines.

YELLOW/GREEN: Fresh or frozen spinach, collard greens, mustard greens, avocados, and turnip greens. Loose-pack spinach in bags is particularly convenient because you can add only what you need to soups, mixed dishes, and pasta. Frozen pepper slices are easily added to dishes, and pre-washed salad greens and raw spinach make quick work of a colorful salad. Look too for pre-cut honeydew melon.

GREEN: Pre-washed and cut broccoli florets and broccoli stems for slaw, and broccoli sprouts, make getting these healthy vegetables much easier. Pre-shredded cabbage for cooking or for slaw and frozen broccoli and cauliflower florets are also widely available.

WHITE/GREEN: If you don't like preparing onions and garlic, you can find pre-chopped garlic in jars and packaged, pre-chopped fresh onion in the produce section. Washed and sliced celery stalks are great for snacking and sliced mushrooms are available packaged and at many supermarket salad bars.

RED: Root Chakra

Family, Prosperity, Material Needs, Survival

"We are like the little branch that quivers during a storm, doubting our strength and forgetting we are the tree - deeply rooted to withstand all of life's upheavals."

~ Dodinsky

This is the oldest chakra in our human evolution and contains information to keep us stable, centered and rooted in reality. As our foundation for survival, it relates to our most basic needs: a sense of trust, personal safety and protection. Located at the base of the spine, this energy center, believed to open downwards, connects us with the energies of the Earth. This is the energy center that propels us forward in life, regardless of challenges that might face us. In her book *Chakra Foods For Optimum Health*, author Deanna M. Minich explains:

"If you'd like to release a fear around eating or feelings of distrust, the root chakra is the place to be. In fact, eating issues stem from the need to protect oneself. Under- or over-eating may cause you to feel scattered or flighty, but the root chakra helps you to feel grounded and in your body so that you can be in the present moment. Assist your root chakra by eating with others in community and honoring your body's instinct on what to eat by dialoguing with your body on food choices. Foods for grounding and protection: Protein, minerals, root vegetables, edible and medicinal mushrooms, red-colored foods."

The Balanced Root Chakra

Red fruit and vegetables are our protectors, allowing us to balance between being vigilant and outgoing at the same time.

We have all heard of a person described as being down-to-earth. It is someone who takes life in stride and is practical in their decision making and their approach to life. A down-to-earth person is sincere; someone with whom you can talk openly and trust your confidence will be safe. With balanced red energy, there is great calmness, a release of past issues, improved self-survival instincts, good circulation, strength and courage. Here are some other words to describe balanced red energy: grounded, vitality, stamina, living life fully, belonging, daring, pride, patient, constant, ambitious, independent, and spontaneous without fear.

Red energy is concerned with all survival issues – mental, emotional and physical. The basics are food, shelter, family and a sense of belonging. If any of these areas need attention, you can use red foods and balance them with other colors. For example, you are moving to a new neighborhood. You might give your children red foods to help make them feel secure with the change, and yellow foods to assure they are focused and mentally alert.

How We See Red: Our Defense Mechanisms

As this is the energy center supporting our most basic safety and survival, it is responsible for the fight or flight defense mechanism which helps us to physically escape danger. In the early days of human evolution, we either fought off threatening animals, played dead or ran away and hid from them. It makes sense that the first chakra supports athletic mechanisms and the body systems that provide structure: the joints, bones, muscles, legs and feet. It also oversees the immune system and skin. In fact, just look at the common red energy expressions we use: "I won't take this lying down." "He's got both feet on the ground." Or if one feels weak: "I don't have a leg to stand on."

The Underactive Root Chakra: Anxious, Vulnerable (Flight)

Running away from feeling scared and anxious turns into depression, a characteristic of an underactive Root Chakra that when balanced helps us feel secure. When we become apathetic and hide out from life, we surrender to fear and we can feel stuck, unable to move forward. Often a person might turn to food and alcohol or cigarettes to feel safe. With these despairing emotions, a person who has given up might neglect proper care of their body and rely upon sugar and fats to feel better. In the long run, those things can make a person feel even worse.

Nutrition plays a huge part in affecting our emotional behavior. Large amounts of sugar and unhealthy starchy carbs can lead to chronic fatigue and depression among other illnesses. It is also important to drink plenty of water.

The Over-Active Root Chakra: Aggressive, Temperamental (Fight)

Today, the stresses from which we need to escape are not the woolly mammoths and saber tooth tigers on our tail, but SUVs, trucks and cars bearing down on us, toxic relationships, job issues, financial burdens, and how about the news! It's whatever threatens our world and everyone defends themselves differently. Some of us act out aggressively, honking our horns, making gestures or yelling back. We literally see red. That's an expression of an overactive Root Chakra using fighting as a defense. Others passively take flight emotionally and hide from it all or allow their personalities to disappear.

The fight defense mechanism manifests If we have too much red and become overly aggressive. The revved up chakra can make us feel so defensive, we're always in attack mode. This behavior comes out as anger, resentment, exploding temper, stepping over others to get ahead to survive. To cool this imbalance down requires upper chakra balancing using calmer colors: green, blue, purple or violet.

Possible Causes Of Imbalance

We are all subconsciously locked into the conditions of our past. The first chakra is the foundation of our mental, emotional and spiritual health. Remember, every single thought, every single occurrence in our lives is stored in the chakras and helps shape our behavior patterns. Early traumas in the first five years of life include difficult birth, abuse, abandonment, divorce or if you have abused others. When this chakra is bogged down with negative residues, we have lack of vitality, depression, anxiety, fear, lack of trust, anger and frustration

Did You Know...?

- Watermelon is a vegetable. It is related to cucumbers, pumpkins and squash.
- Strawberries contain more vitamin C than oranges.
- Watermelon helps control your heart rate.
- Lycopene is a bright red carotene and carotenoid pigment and phytochemical found in tomatoes and other red fruits and vegetables, such as red carrots, red bell pepper and watermelons. This phytochemical has antioxidant value that can help prevent certain illnesses including prostate cancer.
- Strawberries can potentially fight against cancer and aging.
- Cherries help calm your nervous system.
- Apples help your body develop resistance against infections.
- Studies have shown that pomegranates may help the buildup of plaque in the arteries.
- The color of beets comes from betanin, a phytochemical that's thought to bolster immunity.

- For 4,000 years, pomegranates have been symbols of prosperity, hope and abundance.
- During the Persian wedding ceremony, a basket of pomegranates is placed on the ceremonial cloth to symbolize a joyous future.
- Loaded with antioxidants, pomegranates are the new super food. High in vitamin C and potassium, they are a great source of fiber and low in calories.
- In the traditional Jewish custom, the pomegranate is significant as a representation of the commandments of the Torah. This derives from the belief that each pomegranate contains 613 seeds, which is the exact number of the commandments.
- In ancient Roman mythology, beetroot juice was considered an aphrodisiac to Apollo. Aphrodite is said to have eaten beets to retain her beauty, and in folk magic, if a man and woman eat from the same beet, they will fall in love.

RED FOODS

pomegranates • red apples • red grapes • raspberries

• cranberries • cherries • strawberries • watermelon • tomatoes • beets

• radicchio • blood oranges • red bell peppers • red chili peppers

• red potatoes • red onions • radishes • rhubarb

Root vegetables of beige, brown and black earth colors are part of the red foods group. They are defined as vegetables that have an edible root as an extension of the vegetable that grows underground. Even though they are light in color, rutabagas, daikon radishes, turnips and white potatoes with a brown skin are included. There are also root vegetables in the orange section, carrots, for example. Those we'll keep in the orange section because of their distinct orange pigment.

RED FOOD RECIPES

POMEGRANATE GINGER ALE

1 cup pomegranate juice
1 inch fresh ginger root, peeled and thinly sliced
6 cups sugar-free ginger ale, chilled

1. Pour pomegranate juice in large pitcher and add the thinly sliced ginger root.
2. Cover and refrigerate for 4 hours or longer. The longer you let the juice stand with the ginger root the more intense the flavor.
3. Remove the ginger root with slotted spoon. Add the chilled ginger ale and serve immediately over ice.

Yields 4 servings

VEGETARIAN CHILI

1 tablespoon olive oil

1 large onion, chopped

3 large cloves garlic, minced

1 1/2 tablespoons chili powder

2 teaspoons ground cumin

1/2 teaspoon crushed red pepper

1/2 teaspoon smoked paprika

1 1/2 cups vegetable broth

1 1/2 tablespoons reduced-sodium soy sauce

2 14-ounce cans hot chili beans, undrained

1 14-ounce can black beans, rinsed and drained

1 14-ounce can chick peas, rinsed and drained

2 14-ounce cans fire-roasted diced tomatoes, undrained

1 10-ounce package frozen whole kernel corn

1 cup water

2 bay leaves

2 teaspoons dried oregano

1. Heat the oil in large pot over medium heat. Add the onion and garlic; cook and stir until tender, about 3 to 4 minutes. Add the chili powder, cumin, crushed red pepper and paprika; and cook, stirring until spices are slightly toasted and fragrant, about 1 to 2 minutes.

2. Stir in broth and soy sauce. Add chili beans, black beans, and chick peas, tomatoes, corn, and water; mix well. Add bay leaves and oregano and stir to mix.

3. Bring chili to a low boil and cook 10 to 15 minutes, stirring occasionally. Reduce heat and simmer uncovered gently, stirring occasionally, 30 to 40 minutes. Discard bay leaves.

Yields 8 servings

GARDEN GAZPACHO

1 tablespoon olive oil
1/2 cup chopped onion
2 cloves garlic, chopped
5 cups diced tomatoes (about 2 pounds)
1/2 cup water
2 tablespoons tomato paste
2 teaspoons brown sugar
    Salt and pepper to taste
2 tablespoons fresh lemon juice
1 teaspoon Worcestershire sauce
    Hot pepper sauce to taste
1 small cucumber, diced
1/4 cup chopped red onion
1/4 cup chopped celery
    Sour Cream or plain Greek yogurt

1. Heat olive oil in large saucepan over medium heat. Add the onion and garlic; cook and stir until tender, about 4 minutes.
2. Stir in tomatoes, water, tomato paste, sugar, salt and pepper. Bring tomato mixture to a boil. Reduce heat and simmer for 15 minutes.
3. Place half of the soup in a blender or food processor and process until smooth and pour into large bowl. Repeat and pour into bowl with remaining soup.
4. Stir in lemon juice, Worcestershire and hot pepper sauce. Cover and chill in refrigerator.
5. Serve in bowls. Garnish with diced cucumber, red onion, celery and sour cream.

Yields 4 servings

STRAWBERRY BANANA FRUIT SMOOTHIE

1 pint strawberries, cleaned and frozen

1 small banana, peeled, sliced and frozen

1 cup vanilla yogurt

1 cup orange juice

   Honey to taste

1. Combine the fruits, yogurt, orange juice and honey in blender, and blend until smooth.
2. Taste and adjust seasoning.
3. Garnish with strawberry and sprig of mint.

Yields 2 servings

WATERMELON AND FETA CHEESE TOSSED SALAD

1 tablespoon white wine vinegar

1/2 teaspoon crushed red pepper

2 teaspoons honey

   Salt and pepper to taste

1/8 teaspoon minced garlic

3 1/2 pounds watermelon, seeds removed, cut into 1/2 - inch dice
   (about 3 1/2 cups)

2 teaspoons olive oil

8 ounces torn mixed salad greens (about 6 cups)

1/2 cup sliced red onion

1/3 cup crumbled feta cheese

1. Combine vinegar, crushed red pepper, honey, salt, pepper, garlic and 1/4 cup of the watermelon in the food processor.
2. Process until smooth.
3. With machine still running, drizzle in the oil.
4. Chill in a jar until ready to use.
5. Shake well before using.
6. Toss greens with dressing in large bowl. Mound in center of large flat serving dish.
7. Surround with remaining diced watermelon and sprinkle with onion, crumble cheese over salad.
8. Season with additional freshly ground pepper to taste.

Yields 6 servings

MARINATED TOMATOES ARUGULA LINGUINE

3 cups grape tomatoes, halved

3 green onions, thinly sliced

2 cloves garlic, finely minced

2 tablespoons chopped parley

2 tablespoons tapenade

1 teaspoon dried Italian seasoning

   Salt and pepper to taste

2 to 3 tablespoons olive oil

1 pound linguine or other pasta, cooked and drained

2 cups baby arugula

1/4 cup crumbled feta cheese

1. Combine the tomatoes, onion, garlic, parsley, tapenade, Italian seasoning, salt, pepper, and olive oil. Cover and refrigerate at least 2 hours but no longer than 24 hours.
2. Cook linguine as directed on package; drain. Immediately toss with marinated tomato mixture, arugula and feta cheese.
3. Drizzle with additional olive oil if desired.

Yields 6 servings

EASY MARINARA SAUCE

1 tablespoon olive oil
2 large cloves garlic, finely minced
1 medium onion, finely chopped
1 28-ounce can crushed tomatoes
1/2 cup dry red wine
1/2 teaspoon dried thyme
1 teaspoon dried basil, crushed
1/2 teaspoon dried marjoram, crushed
1/4 teaspoon dried oregano, crushed
1/4 teaspoon crushed red pepper
    Salt and pepper to taste
    Pinch brown sugar

1. Heat the oil over low heat in heavy-bottom saucepan.
2. Add garlic and onion and cook until tender, about 10 minutes. Keep heat low and take care not to burn mixture.
3. Add remaining ingredients to saucepan.
4. Simmer, covered, for 1 hour on lowest possible heat, stirring frequently. Serve with your favorite pasta or recipes.

Yields about 4 cups

Meditation To Feel Safe And Secure

Find a quiet, private place where you feel secure and comfortable. You can stand or sit as long as your feet are on the ground. Let your shoulders drop.

Put your hand on your tummy. Breathe gently all the way down into your hips. Feel the gentle rise and fall of your breath, like a wave. With your eyes closed, focus on your breath and the sensation of the inhale and exhale of air. Gently slow down the pace of the breath. Keep breathing deeply into your belly. Let the exhale tumble out like a sigh. Do this five times.

As your breath takes you deeper into a sense of calming comfort, begin to imagine your own special place. It is a place that allows you to feel secure. It is serene, quiet and peaceful. It could be a place familiar to you or one that you imagine or picture. Maybe it is in the beautiful outdoors, or in a special room somewhere. It is a place where there are no intrusions. You are protected in your special place. Allow yourself to go there.

When you are in your special place, notice the time of day, what the weather feels like or the temperature. Perhaps there are sounds you notice, a fragrance or aroma. What do you notice about the touch – the feel of your skin against something in your special place? How does it feel emotionally to be in your special place? Breathe those feelings in and send the breath throughout your body.

Now find the most comfortable, most empowering, connected spot within your special place. Take a few moments to soak up the benefits of being in your special place...let rest, rejuvenation, balance and harmony be yours – and the mind and body will respond.

Open your eyes and stretch.

– Credit: Cheryl O'Neill, C.Ht., American Hypnosis Association, Therapeutic Imagery Program at The Hypnosis Motivation Institute, Tarzana, CA

Please remember, that with all meditations, you cannot be driving a car or operating heavy machinery.

The Quickie Version

The Special Place visualization for relaxation and security can be simplified so that you can use it for just a few minutes at work, at home, or at school.

With your shoulders dropped, your jaw loose, enjoy a relaxed breath. Breathe deeply all the way down to your tummy. Let the breath release from your mouth, gently, like a sigh.

Keep breathing deeply, focusing on the breath and take yourself to your own special place. It is important to imagine you are actually there, using all of your senses: hearing the sounds, feeling the air and the temperature, seeing the colors, smelling the aromas, feeling the peace, slowing life down. Then, when you are ready, come back into your body and take a good stretch.

Meditation To Feel Grounded With The Earth

This is a popular meditation used by hypnotherapists and energy workers. It's great when you feel stressed or light headed or anxious - which means you are living in your head and not grounded with the earth.

Find a quiet, private place where you feel secure and comfortable. You can stand or sit as long as your feet are on the ground.

Let your shoulders drop. Put your hand on your tummy. Breathe gently all the way down into your hips. Feel the gentle rise and fall of your breath, like a wave.

With your eyes closed, focus on your breath and the sensation of the inhale and exhale of air. Gently slow down the pace of the breath. Keep breathing deeply into your belly as though your lungs are in your hips. Let the exhale tumble out like a sigh. Do this five times.

Visualize or imagine roots sprouting out of the bottoms of your feet (or from your spine if you are sitting on the ground). Allow them to sprout slowly and energetically.

Experience what the roots look like. The color. The thickness. The feeling of them growing from your feet or spine. Feel the softness of the earth against your skin.

Now visualize or imagine those roots working their way deep into the soil. Deeper and deeper, until you feel them comfortably connecting with the power of the Earth. The deeper the roots, the more energized and anchored you become.

When you are ready, picture in your mind's eye, or sense your roots connecting with the core of the earth, the heart of our planet. Feel it beating.

Take three slow, deep cleansing breaths, and feel the connection between yourself and the love of Mother Earth. It is as though the roots are the umbilical cord to Mother Earth.

Feel the exchange of energy. Release any old hurts, any discomforts that do not serve you and cleanse your roots with vibrant, healing energy from the Earth.

Allow yourself to linger with this connection as long as you need to. When the time is right, thank Mother Earth for her loving vibration and slowly pull your roots back all the way within. Open your eyes and stretch.

Connect With Earth Energy Physically

Sit at the base of a tree or hug one.
Walk, dance or run barefoot in the grass.
Dig your toes into the sand.
Plant some flowers.
Lie on the ground.
Listen to the Earth's heart beat.

Affirmations

"I am secure and stable, grounded and trusting in my abilities."
"I am safe and secure at all times."
"I allow prosperity into my life."
"I move forward in life with grace and ease."

ORANGE: Sacral Chakra

Creativity, Sensuality, Going With The Flow

"We can let ourselves be carried by the river of feeling because we know how to swim."

~ Jack Kornfield

Unlike the guarded Root Chakra whose job it is to keep you safe and secure, the Sacral Chakra, orange energy, throws caution to the winds and is related to more zest for life – spontaneity and an openness to the world – a sensual wonderment very much like the curiosity of young children. Emotions, including those related to our sexuality, are meant to be felt in full, fueling creativity and self-expression. When you feel free to be who you are and enjoy a passion for life, your Sacral Chakra is vibrating properly and balanced.

Located in the area between your lower abdomen (groin) and your navel, this energy center is where masculine and feminine energies are found. The Sacral Chakra governs our reproductive, urinary and lower digestive system: Sacral body parts include all sexual organs, kidneys, bladder, prostate and spleen. This is also where your attitudes about sexuality are located and feelings about finances. The lower back is your source of physical support. "Oh, my aching back" is all about financial support.

As the Sacral Chakra oversees the liquid functions of the body, it helps you "go with the flow in life." The fulfillment of life's greatest passions, dreams, ambitions and fantasies are possible when this chakra is balanced.

The Balanced Sacral Chakra

A person whose Sacral Chakra is balanced has a natural ability to connect with their feelings and with others with warmth and openness. In other words, relationships come easy. Balanced orange energy helps support motivation - a clear vision of where you want to be and how to get there. To maintain balance, eat orange foods, and use orange aromatherapy extracts. Physically open your hips where orange energy is stored, through dance (how about belly dancing) and strengthen your core with Pilates and yoga. And be sure to have a good belly laugh every day.

The Underactive Sacral Chakra

People who are socially stiff, cold, unresponsive, and inflexible can use more orange. When Sacral Chakra energies are taxed or clogged and spinning slows down, one might become sluggish, uncomfortable with sex, lacking in creative inspiration, cold to others, and they might abandon their dreams.

The Overactive Sacral Chakra

Too much orange energy can cause us to take our "joie de vivre" to the extreme and become addicted to pleasure. Perhaps we have an excessive libido. As a result, we may find ourselves attracting co-dependant relationships. Or, we can be greedy, money hungry, addicted to booze, and overeat.

Did You Know...?

- Yunani and Ayurvedic Medicine have been using honey for thousands of years to strengthen men's fertility.
- In China, Japan and the Far East, women have been taking cinnamon powder for centuries to strengthen the uterus. It is also known to be an aphrodisiac.
- It is believed by some that the bee pollen in the honey prolongs the life of the egg during ovulation.
- Pumpkin seeds are especially beneficial for expectant mothers because of high amounts of protein, zinc and other vitamins.
- Oranges help maintain great skin and vision.
- Mangoes may protect against several kinds of cancer.
- Peaches are rich in potassium, fluoride and iron.
- And how about a navel orange powering the orange chakra? Looks just like a belly button! No coincidence there.
- Carrots were first grown as a medicine.
- The first fruit eaten on the moon was a peach.

Affirmations

"I feel the pleasures of life with every breath I take."
"I am open to touch and closeness."
"I enjoy being in the moment and being spontaneous."
"I am worthy of love and sexual pleasure."
"I can go with the flow and feel secure."

ORANGE FOODS

butternut squash • yams • sweet potato • pumpkin

• honey • carrots • cinnamon • mangoes • papayas

• nuts and seeds • oranges • tangerines • cantaloupe • golden kiwifruit

• nectarines • peaches • apricots • flax seed • paprika • ginger

ORANGE FOOD RECIPES

ROASTED BUTTERNUT SQUASH WITH COCONUT AND LIME SOUP

2 large butternut squash peeled and diced (about 8 cups)

2 tablespoons olive oil

1 teaspoon ground cumin

1 teaspoon ground coriander

1 large onion, chopped

2 1/2 cups vegetable broth

1/4 cup chopped cilantro

1 large onion, chopped

2 teaspoons finely chopped seeded jalapeño

1/4 cup Coconut Milk

    Juice of 1 lime

    Salt and pepper to taste

1. Heat oven to 400 degrees. Place the squash into rimmed cookie sheet. Drizzle with 1 tablespoon olive oil and toss to coat. Spread the squash evenly onto cookie sheet. Roast until slightly browned, about 20 minutes, stirring occasionally. Remove from oven and set aside.
2. Heat remaining 1 tablespoon olive oil in large saucepan over medium-high heat. Add the cumin, coriander, and onion. Cook and stir until onion is tender, about 5 minutes.
3. Add the roasted squash, broth, 2 tablespoons cilantro and jalapeño.
4. Cover and simmer gently until squash is soft, about 20 minutes. Stir Coconut Milk and lime juice. Add more broth if necessary for desired consistency.

Yields 6 servings

Garnish with remaining cilantro.

SWEET POTATO AND KALE CHOWDER

2 tablespoons olive oil

2 cloves garlic, minced

3 celery ribs, chopped

2 medium sweet potatoes, peeled and diced

1 medium red onion, chopped

2 tablespoons minced fresh sage or 1 teaspoon dried

6 1/2 cups broth

1 15-ounce low sodium cannellini beans, rinsed and drained

1 bunch kale, stems trimmed, cut into small pieces, leaves roughly sliced,
   (about 8 ounces)
   Salt to taste

1/4 teaspoon crushed red pepper
   Grated Parmesan cheese

1. Heat the oil in large saucepan or Dutch oven over medium-high heat. Add the garlic, celery, potatoes, onions and sage. Cook and stir until vegetables are tender, about 5 minutes.
2. Add the broth and beans. Cook, covered, until potatoes are tender, about 20 minutes.
3. Stir in kale and crushed pepper. Cook, covered until leaves are tender, about 10 minutes.
4. Serve with Grated Parmesan cheese.

Yields 6 servings

MANGO PINEAPPLE SALSA

1/2 of a medium pineapple, peeled and diced
2 large mangoes, peeled and diced
1/2 small red onion, diced
1/2 red bell pepper, diced
2 jalapeños, seeded and finely chopped
2 tablespoons chopped cilantro
   Juice of 2 limes
2 teaspoons grated ginger
   Salt to taste

1. Combine all the salsa ingredients in bowl.
2. Cover and let stand for about 30 minutes to let flavors marinate.
3. Serve with your favorite chips, grilled fish, or grilled chicken.

Yields about 6 servings

OVEN ROASTED PUMPKIN

1 medium pumpkin, about 5 pounds
1/4 cup olive oil
   Salt to taste
   Mild curry powder, Cajun seasoning, cumin, ground ginger, or Moroccan seasoning (optional)

1. Heat oven to 375 degrees.
2. Wash exterior of pumpkin. Using a large, sharp knife, cut off top just below stem. Then cut in half through the stem end. Scoop out the seeds and fibrous interior. Lay the pumpkin on the cutting board with the cut side down.
3. Carefully remove all of the peel with the knife. Cut the flesh into 1-inch pieces, about 10 cups diced pumpkin.
4. Place the diced pumpkin in a single uncrowded layer in large rimmed baking pan or 2 smaller baking pans. Drizzle with oil and season with the salt and optional seasoning. Gently toss to coat the pumpkin pieces.
5. Roast, stirring often, until the pumpkin is tender and golden, about 40 to 45 minutes.
6. Turn on oven to broil. Broil pumpkin 6 inches from heat source until crisped on one side, about 3 minutes. Cool.

Yields about 6 to 8 servings

TIP: Look for sugar pumpkins (also known as pie pumpkins) for cooking - they have a denser, more tasty flesh than jack-o-lantern pumpkins. You can substitute 2 1/2 pounds peeled, diced butternut squash.

ASIAN CARROT SALAD

4 cups shredded carrots
1/4 cup seasoned rice vinegar
1 tablespoon sesame oil
1 tablespoon sugar
1/4 teaspoon ground ginger

1. Place the carrots in large bowl. In a separate bowl, mix together the vinegar, sesame oil, sugar, and ground ginger with wire or fork until well combined.
2. Pour this dressing over carrots and toss to coat the carrots. Let stand for about 5 to 10 minutes so that the flavors will develop.
3. Serve at room temperature or chilled.

Yields 4 servings

CANTALOUPE GINGERED SMOOTHIE

20 ice cubes

2 cups cubed cantaloupe (about 1/2 medium melons)

6 ounces low-fat plain yogurt

3 tablespoons honey

1/2 teaspoon grated fresh ginger

1. Combine ice cubes, cantaloupe, yogurt, honey, and ginger in blender and purée until smooth.
2. Taste and add more honey if you like.

Yields 3 to 4 servings

Clear Orange Energy With This Belly Exercise

Breathe deeply into your belly. As you do, rub the skin of your belly with your hand in a clockwise direction. Keep taking those slow deep breaths. Meditate on feeling free to express your emotions and follow your dreams.

Increase Energy Flow With A Good Belly Laugh

In addition to stimulating the orange energy responsible for sexuallity, digestive systems are stimulated. It's a great aerobic workout too. Dr. William Fry from Stanford University measured that 20 minutes of laughter is equivalent to 10 minutes on a rowing machine. And according to a study by heart specialists at the University of Maryland, people with heart disease were 40% less likely to laugh in a variety of situations compared to people of the same age without heart disease.

Laughter has been found to benefit the way blood flows around the body, reducing the likelihood of heart disease. Researchers claim that 15 minutes of laughter a day is as important for your heart as 30 minutes of exercise 3 times a week!

Laughter Is Good For You

- Hearty laughter assists in releasing endorphins, natural chemicals that help promote a sense of well-being.
- Stress levels (cortisol) can be reduced by 75%.
- Laughter relaxes tense muscles and they can stay relaxed for up to forty-five minutes.
- The average person laughs thirteen times in a single day.
- A six-year-old child laughs about three times more than an adult.
- Cats and dogs also laugh.
- A hearty laugh is known to decrease stress hormones and increase immune cells and antibodies.
- Laughter can increase blood flow which can help protect against heart attacks.

How To Have A Belly Laugh

Take a private moment and say to yourself out loud, "Hee-hee-heee-hee-hah-hah-hah-hah-hah-ha! Ho-ho-ho-hah-ha-ha-ha-ha!" Do it again, enjoying the sensation of the laughter. Do this several times - feel the belly move! It is suggested that we do belly laughing every day.

Join A Laughter Club

You can also enjoy therapeutic laughter in the company of fellow laughers by joining a Yoga Laughter Club, originally created by Dr. Madan Kataria, a physician in Mumbai India. In his scholarly work, he revealed that laughter is extremely beneficial to mental and physical health. To find a Yoga Laughter Club near you, visit Laughter Yoga International at http://laughteryoga.org/

Laugh With A TV Laugh Track

Laughter is contagious! To get your belly laugh going, simply download a laugh track - the background laughter used in television (*Ultimate Laugh Tracks For Sitcoms, Game Shows, Talk Shows and Comedy Projects, Vol. 2*). They have 50 tracks to choose from. We recommend track 26. It's online at Amazon.com.

Affirmations

"I feel the pleasures of life with every breath I take."
"I am open to touch and closeness."
"I enjoy being in the moment and being spontaneous."
"I am worthy of love and sexual pleasure."
"I enjoy going with the flow."

YELLOW: Solar Plexus Chakra

Self-Esteem, Will Power, Mental Clarity

"You are braver than you believe,
smarter than you seem,
and stronger than you think."

~ Winnie the Poo

Found in your solar plexus, just below the breastbone, and above the navel – *to find it easily, put your hands around your waist* – this is where our conscious thoughts and opinions are formed and controlled. Yellow is the color of the sun and represents your personal power, self-esteem, metabolism and digestion. It is the color of the mental portion of our consciousness that supports thinking, your sense of who you are, the power within you, the power you have over others and the power others have over you. Your gut instinct, which originates in the sensual Solar Plexus Chakra as an emotion, appears here in a more cerebral form.

Yellow relates to ego, our source of identity, our will, sense of self and personal power (setting boundaries). It also stimulates brain power. Good chakra balancing of the Solar Plexus Chakra leads to a healthy ego, recognition and a respect for one's personal power, cheerfulness and enjoyment of new challenges. It is the color that transforms logic and intellect to wisdom, helping you through changes - perhaps different work or a new place to live.

Yellow And Our Physical Body

Yellow energy powers our digestive organs, esophagus, stomach, pancreas, small intestines, liver and gallbladder. You have heard the expressions, "I trust my gut," "I can't stomach that," or "It gives me butterflies in my stomach when I think about it." These are yellow chakra instincts that guide us and direct us to what to do when we need assistance in deciding.

51

The Balanced Solar Plexus Chakra

When we are exposed to sunshine, the day is clear and bright. So, too, our Solar Plexus Chakra shines a light on our mental clarity, allowing us to fulfill several tasks at once. Yellow supports the positive light in which we see ourselves and with appreciation of our self-worth, it helps us to set boundaries. We can use firm kindness, have respect for others as well as ourselves, and take initiative without being overbearing. When we can set an example of being confident and knowledgeable, people look up to us as leaders; we are willing to explore the unknown with confidence and direction.

The Underactive Solar Plexus Chakra

When this chakra is blocked or spinning too slowly, we do not see the sunlight, only the shadow. We see ourselves through the eyes of others, whether we imagine it or it is real. We put ourselves down, take a back seat to others and resent them for it. We can experience shame, anger, fear, bitterness, resentment, prejudice, even hate. In other words we do not have the ego strength to stand up for ourselves. You may recall, in old Westerns, a person who couldn't stand up for himself and others was called "yellow bellied coward." With too little yellow, we have low self-esteem, lack courage to try new things, and become insecure and depressed. We blame others when things do not go our way.

A lack of yellow could result in becoming passive aggressive, rigid, cunning, and overly possessive to compensate for what we are not able to have on our own. Yellow is a color of intellect and wisdom. When we feel lost in our emotions, we cannot access what we already know. Nor do we have the courage to do so.

You may recall, in *The Wizard Of Oz,* the cowardly lion wished to become courageous. Obviously, he had an underactive Solar Plexus Chakra that could be balanced. Dorothy tells him that he already has courage within him.

The Overactive Solar Plexus Chakra

Too much yellow, and everything we like about yellow is amped up and spinning too quickly. When this happens, we can overdo to the extent that we can no longer focus or complete one task at a time. We can become workaholics, perfectionists and overly judgmental of others and demanding. Since this chakra is speeding, we cannot relax for a second.

Another interesting thing happens. Balanced yellow energy supports self-confidence. Too much yellow, and we become egotistical. Very often an inflated ego is due to insecurity and fear. True confidence comes from authentic knowledge of yourself.

Other traits include mentally bullying, always planning and never manifesting, and stubbornness. To balance out overheated yellow, cool it down with cool colors: green or lavender.

Did You Know...?

- Mustard seeds contain flavonoid antioxidants such as carotenes, zeaxanthin and lutein. In addition, the seeds have a small amount of vitamin anti-oxidants such as vitamin A, C and vitamin K.
- The only food that doesn't spoil is honey.
- Pineapples can help fight arthritis.
- Corn always has an even number of rows.
- Lemons contain more sugar than strawberries.
- The banana "tree" is not really a tree, but a giant herb. The banana is the fruit of this herb.
- Lemons will keep for several weeks when refrigerated in a lidded jar.

Dr. Robert E. Svoboday, author of *Ayurveda For Women: A guide to vitality and health*, suggests:

"Immediately before you eat, chew some ginger marinated in lemon or lime juice to awaken your taste buds, to start your juices flowing and to purify your tongue and mouth."

YELLOW FOODS

lemons • yellow summer squash • yellow winter squash • yellow sweet peppers • Yukon Gold potatoes • heirloom yellow tomatoes • sweet corn • yellow apples • yellow beets • yellow figs • yellow pears • yellow peppers • yellow grape tomatoes • pineapple • bananas • grapefruit • yellow lentils • curcumin • turmeric • saffron • mustard spice • ginger • lemon grass

The Importance Of Turmeric And Curcumin

"TheSolar Plexus Chakra is balanced when vibrating at the resonance of the color yellow. Thus, eating the spice curry would be very vibrationally congruent with this energy center and provide the solar plexus with the color frequency it needs..."

~ Deanna Minich at *foodandspirit.com*

Much more than a mere condiment, turmeric is considered as a highly potent medicine and has been extensively used in Indian and Chinese medicine to treat a variety of health conditions. An anti-inflammatory agent, it is believed to be efficacious in the treatment of flatulence, liver inflammation, swollen gums and bruises. Turmeric has gained popularity in recent times, even though it has been used extensively in India since ancient times for flavoring and coloring curries.

Scientists are particularly intrigued with curcumin, the active ingredient in turmeric, common in East Indian curries. Dr. Keith Black of Cedars Sinai in Los Angeles states, "Indians have a lower incidence of Alzheimer's and one theory is that it's the curcumin."

The possibilities of curcumin in treating cancer and Alzheimer's disease are being explored. Turmeric also contains a high level of iron and magnesium and moderate levels of vitamin B6 and potassium, aspects which make turmeric perfect for a balanced diet.

Powdered turmeric is bright yellow and has a distinct earthy aroma and surprisingly pleasing sharp, bitter, spicy lingering flavor. It is a member of the ginger family and like ginger it is the root of the turmeric plant. The color of turmeric comes from curcumin, the yellow-orange pigment and the most important ingredient in turmeric. Turmeric is versatile and lends its flavor to a wide variety of dishes. It is most often associated with curries. It works well in stir-fried vegetables, rice dishes, soups, sauces, stews and teas. Turmeric powder should be stored in an airtight container, away from the light and extreme heat and humidity. It should keep its color and full flavor for 12 to 15 months. Have Turmeric Ginger Tea every morning for a bright sunny day.

YELLOW FOOD RECIPES

TURMERIC GINGER TEA

1/4 teaspoon powdered or ground turmeric
1/4 teaspoon ground ginger
1/2 teaspoon honey
8 ounces hot water

1. Place the turmeric, ginger and honey in coffee cup or mug.
2. Pour in hot water and stir until dissolved. Great in place of coffee.

Yields 1 cup

AZTEC CORN SOUP

5 to 6 medium ears fresh corn*
3 1/2 cups low sodium chicken broth
   Salt to taste
2 fresh poblano chilies, roasted, peeled, seeded and deveined
3 tablespoons butter
1 large tomato, broiled
1/4 cup coarsely chopped onion
1/2 teaspoon dried oregano leaves, crushed
1/2 cup heavy cream

1. Cut corn kernels from cob with knife. Scrape cobs with knife or spoon to remove pulp. Makes about 4 cups combined kernels and pulp.
2. Combine corn, broth, salt in 3 quart saucepan. Bring to a boil over high heat. Reduce to low. Cover and simmer 8 to 10 minutes until corn is tender.
3. Remove 1/2 cup corn from saucepan with slotted spoon; set aside. Place remaining soup, half at a time, in blender and process until smooth. Return to saucepan.
4. Cut chilies lengthwise into 1/2-inch wide strips crosswise into 2 to 3-inch lengths. Cook and stir chilies in butter in medium skillet over medium heat 4 to 5 minutes until chilies are limp and tender. Remove with slotted spoon; set aside. Reserve melted butter in skillet.
5. Place the tomato, onion and oregano in blender, process until smooth. Heat reserve butter over medium heat until hot; add the tomato mixture. Cook and stir 4 to 5 minutes until thickened.
6. Add the tomato mixture in saucepan; bring to a boil over high heat and reduce heat to low and simmer, uncover, 5 minutes.
7. Remove soup from heat; stir in cream. Heat over very low heat about 30 seconds or just until hot. Do not boil. Ladle into bowls. Garnish with reserved corn and chilies, if desired.

Yields 4 to 6 servings

*Substitute two 10-ounce packages frozen whole kernel corn for the fresh corn omitting step 1. In step 2 reduce cooking time to 4 to 5 minutes.

VEGETABLE CORN SALAD

4 cups cooked corn kernels
1 small yellow squash, diced
1 small zucchini, diced
1/2 medium red bell pepper, diced
4 green onions, thinly sliced
2 tablespoons chopped cilantro
1/4 cup olive oil
   Juice of 1 lemon or lime
2 to 3 teaspoons ground cumin
   Salt and pepper to taste

1. Place the corn, yellow squash, zucchini, red bell pepper, green onion and cilantro in large bowl. Toss to combine the vegetable mixture.
2. Drizzle with olive oil and lemon juice.
3. Add the cumin, salt and pepper. Toss well to combine ingredients.
4. If desired chill or serve at room temperature on bed of lettuce.

Yields 6 servings

ROASTED YELLOW BEET SALAD

1 pound yellow beets, stems trimmed

1 tablespoon minced shallots or sweet onion

1 tablespoon fresh lemon juice

3 tablespoons fresh orange juice

1 teaspoon grated orange rind

1/2 teaspoon Dijon mustard

1 tablespoon olive oil

    Salt to taste

1 5-ounce package arugula, or other mixed greens

1/3 cup crumbled goat or feta cheese

1/4 cup thinly sliced red onion or sweet onion

1. Heat the oven to 400 degrees.
2. Rinse the beets and pat dry with paper towel. Place the beets on rimmed baking pan and roast until tender, about 45 minutes; cool.
3. Peel and dice the beets.
4. Whisk together the shallots, lemon juice, orange juice, rind and mustard. Whisk in the oil until emulsified and season with salt to taste.
5. Arrange the salad greens, beets, cheese, and onion on 4 individual salad plates. Drizzle each salad with the dressings. Serve immediately.

Yields 4 servings

LEMON VINAIGRETTE

2 tablespoons white wine vinegar
2 tablespoons fresh lemon juice
1 teaspoon Dijon mustard
1 teaspoon lemon zest
1 teaspoon honey or agave
1/2 teaspoon sea salt
1/4 teaspoon ground white pepper
   Dash garlic powder
2/3 cup olive oil

1. Combine the vinegar, lemon juice, mustard, lemon zest, honey, salt, pepper, and garlic powder in medium bowl, whisking to blend.
2. Gradually add the olive oil in thin stream, whisking constantly until well blended and smooth. Adjust seasoning if needed.

Yields about 1 cup

YUKON GOLD GARLIC POTATOES

1 pound small Yukon potatoes (unpeeled)
1 tablespoon butter
1 tablespoon olive oil
4 large cloves garlic, finely minced
     Salt and pepper
1/4 cup chopped parsley

1. Cook potatoes in lightly salted water until tender, about 15 minutes. Drain and cool.
2. Cut potatoes into quarters and set aside. Melt the butter with the olive oil in large heavy skillet over medium heat.
3. Add the potatoes and cook 5 minutes, stirring frequently. Increase heat to high. Cook potatoes until deep golden brown, turning frequently, about 10 minutes.
4. Add the garlic, salt, pepper, and parsley. Continue to cook for a few minutes. Serve hot.

Yields 6 servings

SAUTEED YELLOW SQUASH AND ONIONS

1 tablespoon olive oil
4 medium yellow squash, cut into 1/4-inch slices
1/2 medium onion sliced
1 medium garlic, finely chopped
1 tablespoon chopped fresh dill weed
    Salt and pepper to taste
    Juice of 1/2 of a lemon

1. Heat the olive oil in large skillet over medium-high heat until hot. Add the onion and garlic; cook and stir until slightly tender, about 2 to 3 minutes.
2. Add the yellow squash, dill weed, salt and pepper. Continue cooking until tender, about 5 minutes
3. Squeeze lemon juice into squash mixture and gently toss to coat the vegetables. Serve immediately.

Yields 6 servings

BANANA PINEAPPLE COCONUT SMOOTHIE

2 bananas, peeled, sliced and frozen

1 1/2 cups diced fresh pineapple, frozen

1 cup vanilla yogurt

1/2 cup shredded coconut

1 to 2 tablespoons honey

Place bananas, pineapple, yogurt, coconut and honey in blender. Blend until smooth.

Yields 2 to 3 servings

De-Stress Ritual Before Cooking And Eating

How much yellow do you have going on? Do you act like a turtle when you are stressed. Do you retreat into your shell? Or do you stick your neck out too far?

Right now, notice the position of your shoulders. Are they raised up? If they are, let them drop. Doesn't that feel good? We subconsciously raise our shoulders up when we're stressed or fearful. It is a defensive reflex. It could be when we're at the computer, driving, or even watching a cliffhanger on TV, we get into this "turtle pose."

Thing is, it's tough for the body to release the appropriate enzymes and metabolize your food when your body is on alert for combat or to run. So before cooking and eating, throw a couple of imaginary bean bags on your shoulders to enhance your metabolism.

Bean Bags On Your Shoulders

With your eyes closed, visualize or imagine bean bags placed upon both of your shoulders. Notice how your shoulders drop. Take a full breath and feel the empowerment of having your shoulders relaxed, yet squarely facing life and all its events. Enjoy five more deep breaths in this moment.

Affirmations

"I can assert myself and feel comfortable with my own power."
"I value myself and know what is best for me."
"I am enough, I am complete."
"I know I am able make my life work."
"I allow myself to seek the life I want."

GREEN: Heart Chakra

Love, forgiveness, compassion

"Be kind, for everyone you meet is fighting a hard battle."

~ Philo

The Heart Chakra is located on the spine behind the breast bone, between the shoulder blades. This is the chakra that supplies you with all of the information you've collected in all lifetimes about love, spirituality, and compassion.

The Heart Chakra And Our Physical Body

The Heart Chakra is responsible for circulatory functions of the body, such as the heart, lungs, lymphatic system, and blood vessels. This includes the nurturing functions of the body through the breast, shoulders, arms, hands and fingers.

The Balanced Heart Chakra

When your heart is open, you have self-love, forgiveness and enjoy the company of others without being needy. You are able to give and receive love in equal proportions.

The Underactive Heart Chakra

When this chakra spins too slowly or is out of balance, it can make us feel unworthy of love, heighten fear of rejection and a fear of letting go. To protect ourselves we become withdrawn, cold, distant and distrusting. Other traits are envy, inability to forgive, and isolation from feelings. Interestingly enough, the expression "green with envy" goes back to the early Greeks who thought when someone was jealous, the body produced too much bile, making their skin a greenish tint.

The Overactive Heart Chakra

The very opposite of being withdrawn is chasing after love to excess. When we have a gaping hole in our heart, it is empty of love and we are desperate to fill it. We are so hungry for love that we roll over to please everyone, even if it doesn't benefit us. In fact, "no" is not even in our vocabulary. It is as if our actions are saying: "Please love me." In relationships, there is a tendency to give your all to an unappreciative partner who doesn't give anything in return.

Did You Know...?

- Celery has high amounts of vitamin C for a healthy immune system. Celery also has calming properties.
- For centuries, celery has been used as a diuretic to flush out excess fluid from the body.
- Celery contains coumarins shown to be effective in cancer prevention.
- There are anti-inflammatory properties in celery that might aid arthritis sufferers.
- Green foods contain the chemicals sulforaphane and isocyanate, and they also contain indoles, all of which can help ward off cancer by inhibiting carcinogens.
- Chlorophyll, the molecule that gives green plants their pigments, may speed up healing, nourish the bone marrow and enrich the blood.
- Cucumbers contain most of the vitamins you need every day. Just one cucumber contains Vitamin B1, Vitamin B2, Vitamin B3, Vitamin B5, Vitamin B6, Folic Acid, Vitamin C, Calcium, Iron, Magnesium, Phosphorus, Potassium and Zinc.
- To avoid a hangover or headache, eat a few cucumber slices before going to bed.
- Cucumbers contain enough sugar, B vitamins and electrolytes to replenish essential nutrients the body lost, keeping everything in equilibrium.
- Lettuce and celery will keep longer if stored in the refrigerator in paper bags instead of cellophane ones. Do not remove the outside leaves of either until ready to use.
- According to University of Illinois researcher Frances "Ming" Kuo, staying in touch with nature is essential for good health. "Much like eating greens provides essential nutrients, so does seeing and being around green." A study from the University of Essex England claims you can boost your mood and sense of well-being walking in a city park, cycling in green outdoor surroundings, and gardening, for as little as five minutes a day.

- Green tea has 200 times the antioxidant power of vitamin E. It works best when you brew the tea loose instead of using a tea bag. Unlike coffee, green tea hydrates you.
- Green tea's anti-oxidant properties, particularly epigallocatechin (EPCG), inhibits the growth of cancer cells and it kills cancer cells without causing any harm to healthy tissue. Researchers at the USDA reported that green tea also produces greater antioxidant activity than 22 commonly consumed fruits and vegetables.
- Steaming broccoli for two to four minutes preserves anti-cancer enzymes and nutrients.
- Hugging your pet with genuine love and affection can help balance your Heart Chakra.
- Hippocrates noted the medicinal properties of lettuce in 430 B.C.
- One-third pound stalk of broccoli contains more vitamin C than 204 apples.

GREEN FOODS

artichokes • arugula • asparagus • avocados • broccoflower • broccoli
• broccoli rabe • brussels sprouts • bok choy • chayote squash
• cabbage • chinese cabbage • cucumbers • green apples • green beans
• green cabbage • green grapes • green onion • green pears • green peppers
• honeydew • kiwifruit • leafy greens • lettuce • limes
• okra • peas • snow peas • spinach • sugar peas • olives • watercress
• zucchini • cauliflower and other cruciferous vegetables
• kale • parsley • basil • rosemary • thyme

WHITE/GREEN FOODS

Leeks •scallions • garlic • onions • celery • pears • white wine • endive • chives

GREEN FOOD RECIPES

SAUTEED ARUGULA, SPINACH AND TOMATOES

1/4 cup olive oil

4 shallots, thinly sliced

2 cloves garlic, thinly sliced

1 pint grape tomatoes

1 pound spinach, trimmed and washed

1 5-ounce bag arugula, washed

    Salt to taste

1/4 cup finely grated Parmesan cheese

1. Heat the oil in large skillet over medium-high heat. Add the shallots and garlic, cook and stir until soft and starting to brown, about 4 minutes.
2. Add the tomatoes and cook and stir until tomato skins are split, about 2 minutes.
3. Gradually add the spinach, arugula, and salt, cook and stir until tender, about 3 minutes.
4. To serve, sprinkle with Parmesan cheese.

Yields 4 servings

BRAISED COLLARD GREENS CAJUN-STYLE

2 large bunches collards (about 2 pounds), washed and drained
4 cups water
1 medium onion, thinly sliced
4 to 5 cloves garlic, minced
1/2 teaspoon crushed red pepper
2 tablespoons olive oil
1 cup vegetable or chicken broth
1 large tomato, diced
2 to 3 teaspoons brown sugar (optional)
1/2 to 1 teaspoon hot sauce
    Dash cayenne
    Salt to taste

1. Remove and discard the woody stem from greens. Stack the collard leaves, a few at a time, and roll. Cut them crosswise into 1/4-inch-wide strips.
2. Bring salted water to a boil in large saucepan or Dutch oven. Add the collards, cover and cook over medium heat stirring often until greens are slightly tender, about 15 minutes. Drain greens well.
3. Cook and stir drained greens, onion, garlic and crushed red pepper in olive oil over medium-high heat until tender about 5 minutes.
4. Add the broth, cover and cook over medium heat for about 8 to 10 minutes, until soft.
5. Add remaining ingredients and continue cooking until greens are done, about 8 minutes, stirring occasionally.

Yields 6 servings

CUCUMBER, CARROT AND ONION SALAD

1/4 cup rice vinegar

2 tablespoons sesame oil

2 tablespoons sesame seeds

   Sea salt and pepper to taste

1 cup packaged shredded carrots

1 English cucumber, peeled, seeded, diced

1/2 small red onion, thinly sliced

1. Whisk together vinegar, sesame oil, sesame seeds, salt and pepper in small bowl.
2. Combine carrots, cucumber and onion in medium bowl. Add vinegar dressing, toss to combine thoroughly.

Yields 4 servings

ASPARAGUS RISOTTO

1/2 cup minced onions
3 tablespoons olive oil
2 cups Arborio rice
1 bay leaf
4 cups hot chicken stock
1/2 cup dry white wine
1 cup asparagus purée*
2 tablespoons butter
1/4 cup grated Parmesan cheese
   Salt and pepper to taste

1. Cook and stir onions in the olive oil over medium-high heat in 2 quart saucepan until tender.
2. Add the rice and bay leaf and stir until the rice absorbs all the liquid.
3. Combine the hot stock and wine. Add the stock mixture in 2 ounce increments, stirring constantly between the increments.
4. When the rice is about 3/4 cooked, about 15 minutes, add the asparagus purée, sliced asparagus, butter and Parmesan cheese. Continue to stir until rice is al dente. Season with salt and pepper. Serve with additional grated Parmesan cheese if desired.

Yields 6 servings

*To Make Asparagus Purée: Place 2 bunches Jumbo asparagus (clean and trimmed) in boiling water until slightly tender, about 3 to 4 minutes. Then shock the asparagus by placing it in ice water bath; drain. Set aside 2 spears and thinly slice. Place the asparagus in food processor and purée until smooth, season with salt and pepper to taste.

RAW KALE SALAD

2 pounds curly kale, washed and stems removed
1/2 small red onion, thinly sliced
1/2 small red bell pepper, cut into thin strips
1 clove garlic, finely minced
1 tablespoon grated fresh ginger
2 to 3 tablespoons olive oil
    Juice of 1 lemon or more to taste
2 teaspoons lite soy sauce
    Dash cayenne
    Salt to taste

1. Place the kale in food processor, and coarsely chop. Place in large bowl.
2. Add the onion, red bell pepper, garlic, and ginger.
3. Drizzle with olive oil, lemon juice, and soy sauce. Toss to coat the vegetables. Season with cayenne and salt to taste.

Yields 6 servings

ROASTED KALE CHIPS

2 bunches kale
2 tablespoons olive oil
2 large cloves garlic, minced
    Sea salt and freshly ground black pepper
1 tablespoon toasted sesame seeds

1. Preheat oven to 375°F. Rinse kale and pat dry thoroughly. Remove and discard thick ribs and roughly chop leaves.
2. Pat leaves dry again. Toss with olive oil, garlic, salt and pepper in a large bowl.
3. Spread on a large rimmed baking sheet. Kale does not need to be in a single layer, as it will shrink in volume as it cooks.
4. Bake for 15 to 20 minutes, stirring every five minutes or so, until leaves are tender, crisp on edges and slightly browned. Sprinkle with sesame seeds before serving.

Yields 4-6 servings

MINT PESTO

3/4 cup packed fresh mint leaves

1/4 cup fresh parsley

2 green onions, thickly sliced

2 medium cloves garlic

1/2 teaspoon finely grated lemon zest

2 tablespoons olive oil

    Dash cayenne

    Sea salt to taste

2 tablespoons finely chopped walnuts

1. Combine the mint leaves, parsley, green onions, garlic and lemon zest in a food processor. Pulse until chopped.
2. With the machine on, add the olive oil in a thin stream and process until smooth.
3. Season with dash of cayenne and salt to taste. Stir in walnuts.

Yields about 1/2 cup

Best Uses: Toss the pesto with pasta, mix it with goat cheese and spread on crostini. Also great on roasted, grilled or steamed vegetables.

SESAME BROCCOLI SALAD

1 tablespoon toasted sesame seeds
1 1/2 pounds broccoli, cut into florets, with stems peeled and coarsely chopped
1/2 small red bell pepper, cut in thin strips
1 tablespoon soy sauce
2 tablespoons rice vinegar or white wine vinegar
1 tablespoon sesame or peanut oil
2 teaspoons honey

1. Bring about 2 cups unsalted water to a boil in a large saucepan. Add the broccoli, cover and cook for 5 minutes or until tender but still crisp. Drain in a colander, rinse under cold running water to stop the cooking, and drain again. Transfer to a serving dish.
2. Combine the soy sauce, vinegar, sesame oil and honey. Place the drained broccoli and red bell pepper in large bowl. Pour dressing over broccoli mixture and toss well to combine. Sprinkle with the sesame seeds and serve.

Yields 4 servings

Green Energy Balancing Tips

Go on a nature hike.
Put plants in your home and office.
Do some gardening.
Grow your own herbs.

A Handy Exercise For Your Heart Chakra

Rub your hands vigorously together to open up Heart Chakra energy. You might even clap a few times. Great to do before you start cooking.

Hand Clapping Has Its Rewards

"Over 6,000 years ago, ancient sages discovered hand clapping strengthens lungs and heart. When we strike our palms together forcefully, it activates the pressure points on our palms. This offers numerous health benefits because the clapping produces sound waves that energize the atmosphere, strengthen blood cells and enhance our immunity."

- www.timeswellness.com

Affirmations

"I give and receive love openly and fully."
"I forgive myself and others and release the past."
"I love myself for who I am and the possibilities within me."
"I deeply and truly approve of myself."
"I live my life doing the highest good."

The Forgiveness Meditation

The awful part about resentments is we have a subconscious urge to replay them over and over again. The mind cannot distinguish between what we imagine and what is real, so you may physically experience discomfort as well. To diffuse this habit, you need to get out of your head and shift your focus to your body instead. Here's a meditation to melt hurts:

Sitting in a chair, focus on your breath as you breathe deeply into your hips. Let your exhale tumble out like a sigh. Do this five times.

Starting with your head, send the breath to melt the tension wherever it exists in your body. The neck, shoulders and arms, torso, belly, hips, thighs, knees, calves and feet.

Releasing, relaxing, letting go. Allow a feeling of security and serenity to fill those areas, wherever breath touches...you can feel the tightness dissolving and draining out through your feet.

Now, there is a light within you; it could be a pin dot or a bright beam. As you focus on your breath, allow that light to appear. It exists. It is there. How big or small is it? It is there. You can locate it. It is the love in your being. Perhaps it is hidden behind hurt or resentment. If so, what is the shape of the hurt? What is the color? Imagine the edges of it shrinking, shrinking, shrinking, allowing the light behind it to shine. The brighter the light, the smaller the resentment becomes.

Allow the light to become larger and larger as the hurt or resentment grows smaller. When you feel it is large enough to share, send the love light out to the world.

Suggested Reading: How To Forgive When You Can't, by Dr. Jim Dincalci, Founder of The Forgiveness Foundation

AQUAMARINE: Throat Chakra

Expressing Your Truth

"Unexpressed emotions will never die. They are buried alive and will come forth later in uglier ways."

~ Sigmund Freud

Located on the spine near the collarbone at the lower neck, this chakra affects your throat, neck, mouth, teeth, ears and thyroid gland and contains information about communication. It also is linked to the shoulders, hands and arms. The jaw is where anger is stored and released.

The Balanced Throat Chakra

When you believe you have the right to be heard and that you can speak freely, your words have value and your chakra has equilibrium. Good balancing for this energy center requires fluids to encourage a flow of thoughts through the throat and mouth. Water is the major source of flushing out old hurts and toxic thoughts. Liquids moisten the mouth and throat allowing one's true feelings to be heard. Other liquid nourishments are found in the next few pages.

The Underactive Throat Chakra

So often we feel stifled in situations that make us feel small and we become shy. We swallow our emotions – you've heard of swallowing one's pride, or having a lump in the throat or being tongue-tied – those are metaphors for stuffing emotions down. We do that many ways: overeating, smoking, and drinking. Some say these habits that have to do with the mouth indicate anger towards one's mother or caregiver from infanthood. You can notice how tightlipped people are sealing their lips so that their true feelings don't come out. They are stubborn, resistant to change and critical of others. And they do not hear their own inner voice.

These habits suppress hurts both old and new. When we are fearful about speaking up, saying what we really feel, we shut down our essence. Our ego disappears and we use silence and passive aggression as protection.

Author Karol K. Truman states in her book, *Feelings Buried Alive Never Die*, that it is important to speak your truth otherwise "negative feelings remain very much in your body and these feelings affect each day of your life." (By the way, her book gives excellent, information about thought as energy and its effects. We recommend it highly.)

The Overactive Throat Chakra

When the spinning Throat Chakra spins to excess, we become overly talkative, not letting anyone get a word in edgewise.

"Water Is The Soul Of The Earth."

~ Robert A. Swanson and W.H. Auden

On a spiritual level, the mystical sparkling fluid we call water is symbolic in fables and dreams. In fact, water is spirituality connected in different religions and cultures – from baptism to feng shui. On a physical level, water, the silky liquid life-giving force, quenches our thirst and detoxifies our body. It's our primary source of survival. We need clear, pure water to hydrate our bodies and keep functions balanced properly. Yet, water, the wonder that washes away toxins and keeps our harmonic energetic flow, has become a neglected nutrient in modern society. How many of us actually drink enough water to keep us from dehydration?

According to the article "Depressed Or Dehydrated?" author Jackie Kosednar states:

"It is estimated that 85% of the population experience regular periods of dehydration or are chronically dehydrated. When suddenly hydrated after a lifetime of drought, the body and brain become happy. Although many types of purified, altered waters are very good, curing the dehydration is what helps create the amazing results...water is a vital conductor of energy and electricity. Your cells and nerves, your meridian and chakra energy systems — all need water to function correctly. Dehydration weakens the body by weakening these systems." – http://www.alaskawellness.com/jan-feb2011/dehydrated.htm

How Much Water Do We Have To Drink To Power The Chakras?

It is said that we need to drink half our body weight in ounces of pure natural water every day. If you weigh one hundred and fifty pounds, then you would drink 75 ounces or about 9 glasses of water a day. It might be easier to drink water from a quart bottle. Then you would drink two of them a day.

Water Can Chase Away The Blues

The brain is 76% water. When it is depleted, depression can result. Ongoing studies are investigating the link between depression and dehydration. Remember, water is a conduit for the electrical impulses of the chakra system. Every energy center becomes underactive when we are dehydrated. According to an article from Natural News.com written by Andreas Moritz:

"The human body is composed of 75 percent water and 25 percent solid matter. To provide nourishment, eliminate waste and conduct all the trillions of activities in the body, we need water. Most modern societies, however, no longer stress the importance of drinking water as the most important 'nutrient' among nutrients. Entire population groups are substituting water with tea, coffee, alcohol and other manufactured beverages. Many people don't realize that the natural thirst signal of the body is a sign that it requires pure, plain drinking water. Instead, they opt for other beverages in the belief that this will satisfy the body's water requirements. This is a false belief."

You might be surprised to know that caffeine, alcohol and sugary beverages (even those with artificial sweeteners) can dehydrate you and make you jittery and stressed. When you are parched for peace, security and wisdom to defend yourself, you may withhold your words and become more fearful and not have a voice at all. The Throat Chakra, fueled by lubrication from water – whether you drink it plain or with lemon, cucumber, or mint or as part of a smoothie, or broth or soup, is one of the most important chakras to keep balanced.

According to Dr. F. Batmagnhelidj, author of the landmark book, *Your Body's Many Cries For Water*, we need to drink a minimum of six to eight glasses a day. He suggests:

"One glass half an hour before taking food – breakfast, lunch, and dinner – and a similar amount two-and-a half hours after each meal. For the sake of not shortchanging your body, two more glasses of water should be taken around the heaviest meal or before going to bed."

Five Advantages Of Drinking Water In The Morning

1. Balances your lymph system. These glands help you perform your daily functions, balance your body fluids and fight infection.

2. Glowing skin. Water helps to purge toxins from the blood which help keeps your skin radiant and clear.

3. Helps with weight loss. Drinking at least 16 ounces of chilled water can boost your metabolism by 24% in the morning.

4. Increases the production of new blood and muscle cells.

5. Drinking water on an empty stomach purifies the colon making it easier to absorb nutrients.

– http://undergroundhealthreporter.com

Did You Know...?

- Drinking ice water throughout the day gets the metabolism to work harder because it has to convert cold water to body temperature.
- Drinking hot or warm water after a meal won't allow fats to congeal. It's good to have soup after a meal. Or herbal tea instead of coffee.
- Coconut water has the same electrolyte balance as our blood plasma.
- One serving of coconut water has more potassium than two bananas.

AQUAMARINE FOODS

Aquamarine foods refer to the sea: water and sea vegetables. As the Throat Chakra requires liquids to moisten and lubricate the throat and help facilitate speech, the foods for this chakra are: water, teas, broths, ices, fruit juices, and sea plants/vegetables. You can use fruit juices of any color.

AQUAMARINE RECIPES

EASY MISO SOUP

3 1/3 cups water
1 1/2 ounces dried seaweed
4 tablespoons miso paste with dash stock
1/2 cup diced firm tofu
   Thinly sliced green onions

1. Bring water to a boil in medium saucepan. Add seaweed a little at a time and boil for 3 minutes.
2. Turn off heat and gently dissolve the miso paste in water.
3. Reheat the soup and add the tofu. Turn off heat as soon as water starts to boil. Add the green onions and serve hot.

Yields 3 servings

SEAWEED SALAD

3/4-ounce dried Wakame seaweed (whole or cut)

3 tablespoons rice vinegar (unseasoned)

3 tablespoons soy sauce

1 tablespoon sesame oil

1 teaspoon sugar

1/2 teaspoon wasabi powder or to taste

2 teaspoons finely grated ginger

1 small clove garlic, finely minced

3 green onions, thinly sliced

1 small carrot, cut into small strips

2 tablespoons chopped fresh cilantro

1 tablespoon toasted sesame seeds

1. Cover seaweed with warm water in bowl, and let soak for 5 minutes. Drain in colander, rinse then squeeze out excess water. If Wakame is uncut, cut into 1/2-inch wide strips.
2. Combine vinegar, soy sauce, sesame oil, sugar, wasabi powder, ginger and garlic in bowl. Add the seaweed, green onions, carrot and cilantro. Toss to combine well. Sprinkle with toasted sesame seeds.

Yields about 4 servings

STRAWBERRY BASIL GREEN TEA

1/2 pound washed hulled strawberries
1 tablespoon fresh lemon juice
3 tablespoons honey
1 sprig basil (about 8 leaves)
3 cups iced green tea

1. Place the strawberries, lemon juice, honey, and basil in blender. Blend until smooth, about 30 seconds.
2. Cover and chill until ready to serve.
3. Stir the blended strawberry mixture and green tea together in a pitcher, just before serving.
4. Serve it immediately and stir just before refilling glasses.

Yields 4 servings

FLAVORED ICE CUBES

Flavored ice cubes are great way to add flavor and nutrients to your water. Try adding sliced fruit or diced fruit, veggies or herbs to your ice tray. Then fill tray with water and place in freezer for at least 4 hours before using. There are unlimited combinations you can try.

Place your favorite diced fruits, herbs, mint, citrus, or combination of ingredients in empty ice cube tray. Fill with water, coconut water, or fruit juice and freeze until solid, about 2 hours.

Suggested Combinations:

Lemon and Mint
Pineapple Coconut Cherry
Strawberry Rosemary
Blueberry Lemon
Lavender Lemon
Orange Mango Mint
Green and Red Grapes
Mango Pineapple
Lemon Thyme
Lavender Mint

FRUIT ICE POPS

Want another fun way to enjoy water? How about homemade Fruit Ice Pops. They're made of fruits and herbs. Here are a couple for you to try. Then come up with your own. There are so many combinations!

LEMON BERRY ICE POPS

Juice of 1 fresh lemon
2 cups water
1 cup blueberries, raspberries, chopped strawberries or mixture
   Natural sweetener to taste (such as honey, agave, stevia or maple syrup)
   Ice pop molds
   Ice pop sticks

1. Pour fresh lemon juice into the water.
2. Sweeten lemon water to taste with natural sweetener.
3. Fill molds 2/3 full with lemonade.
4. Freeze uncovered about 1 hour.
5. Take Fruit Ice Pops out. Scrape and stir any ice crystals that have formed.
6. Add a spoonful of berries to mold; be sure to leave a tiny bit of room at the top of your mold, so they don't overflow when you add the stick.
7. With an ice pop stick or butter knife press the berries into mixture, so they are evenly distributed.
8. Add the ice pops sticks and freeze until solid, about 3 to 4 hours.

Yields about 3 cups mixture (about 6 to 7 Fruit Ice Pops)

STRAWBERRY BASIL ICE POPS

Juice of 1 fresh lemon

2 cups water

   Natural sweeter to taste (such as honey, agave, stevia or maple syrup)

1 cup chopped strawberries

2 tablespoons julienned fresh basil

   Ice pop molds

   Ice pop sticks

1. Pour fresh lemon juice into the water.
2. Sweeten lemon water to taste with natural sweetener.
3. Fill molds 2/3 full with lemonade.
4. Freeze uncovered about 1 hour.
5. Take Fruit Ice Pops out. Scrape and stir any ice crystals that have formed.
6. Combine the strawberries and basil together in small bowl. Add a spoonful of strawberry mixture to mold; be sure to leave a tiny bit of room at the top of your mold, so your mixture doesn't overflow when you add the stick.
7. With an ice pop stick or butter knife press the strawberry mixture into lemon mixture, so they are evenly distributed.
8. Add the ice pop sticks and freeze until solid, about 3 to 4 hours.

Yields about 3 cups mixture (about 6 to 7 Fruit Ice Pops)

"Toning" Helps Release Emotions That Are Stuck

When you want to use your voice to express your feelings but feel stuck, do some "toning." Go to a quiet place, lie down on your back, and breathe all the way into your hips so your belly moves up and down like a wave. Breathe deeply, in and out. When an emotion that doesn't serve you comes up, on the exhale, loudly say, "AHHHHHHH," pressing your belly down as long as you can – until the sound becomes a whisper. This is a way to clear suppression or release emotions you have stuffed down inside.

Change Energy By Changing Your Words

Every word that we speak, hear or think creates an emotional and physical response. Each and every word. Not just some words. The emotional response takes place without our conscious awareness because our emotions are rooted in the subconscious.

When we consciously watch the words we use, recognizing their harm, and replace negative words with positive words, then we will champion our right to enjoy happiness. We will no longer stimulate negative images and will no longer experience the negative feelings, attitudes and physical responses associated with that word. You might be surprised to find that the more conscious you are of the words you use, the more positive the whole world appears to you.

Correct Yourself By Replacing Negative Words With Positive Ones

"Do or do not, there is no try."

- Yoda

Replace the words "difficult" and "problem" with "challenging." The words "difficult" and "problem" suggest a struggle - something negative and draining. The word "challenging" suggests a risk and a payoff or maybe a goal.

To "try" is to lie. It implies defeat and programs failure. It is an ideal way to escape responsibility. How easy it is to get around commitment to an answer of yes or no. Drop the word from your vocabulary. Use "I will" or "I will do my best" instead.

"Hope" is a surrender to helplessness and the belief we cannot fulfill our own needs. Using the word hope leads to disappointment and promotes a feeling of anxiety - the subtle dread that something bad is about to happen. It indirectly suggests you need help from others. Replace "hope" with the words "I have confidence" or "I trust" or "I am optimistic." It gives a commitment and provides security.

The word "should" implies punishment. Replace it with the words "I'd like to" which suggest a goal and a desire without pressure. In the *You Can Heal Your Life Workbook*, author Louise Hay states, "...I believe that 'should' is one of the most damaging words in our language. Every time we use should, we are in effect saying 'wrong.' Either we are wrong or we were wrong or we are going to be wrong. I don't think we need more wrongs in our life. We need to have more freedom of choices."

THREE POWERFUL WORDS
OPEN THE DOOR TO A POSITIVE OUTCOME

"UP UNTIL NOW"

Doubts. Fears. Misgivings. Hesitations. Whether we think them silently or say them out loud, we are sending messages to our subconscious mind. One way to tell the subconscious mind to make the change is to add the words "up until now" at the end of the sentence.

For example:

I never could do that....up until now.

I don't have the energy I used to...up until now.

I just can't...up until now.

I can't lose weight...up until now.

I always eat too many cookies...up until now.

That never happens to me ...up until now.

I have never been lucky......up until now.

Practice using this re-programming technique here with your own thoughts:

I _____

I _____

I _____

Be mindful of what you say and remember to use these three powerful words. You will see a difference in how the world reacts to you.

Re-Programming Exercises

Write out on piece of paper a sentence using the negative word. Underneath it, write the same sentence substituting the positive word. Here are examples:

Change This	**To This**
"Paying my bills is difficult."	"Paying my bills is challenging."
"I hope I pass my exams."	"I am optimistic I will pass my exams."
"I will try to do better."	"I will do better."

And how many times do we use the word "should"? It implies an inherent punishment or threat. Imagine not using should, how much lighter you feel.

The following exercise is from Louise Hay's *You Can Heal Your Life Workbook*.

To get to the bottom of "shoulding" fill in the blanks in the sentences below.
I should_____
I should_____
I should_____
Then, after they are filled in, ask yourself "Why?" after each one.
I should _____because _____

Now, re-read the above list one item at a time, except this time begin each sentence by saying:
If I really wanted to, I could _____
Now ask yourself, "Why haven't I?" _____
_____

"I am" are the two most powerful words in our vocabulary because they identify who we are. *I am Pat. I am Charlotte. I am a teacher. I am French. I am 10 years old. I am an owner of cats. I am a redhead. I am a fan of jazz.*

When you say, "I am sorry" those words define you just as you say your name. They become your identity and who you are as a person. That can be harmful because shame also becomes a part of who you are. And the remedy for shame? Punishment. It is one thing to feel sorry than to be sorry because feeling sorry is not all of you – it's only a feeling.

Instead of making it all about you, simply express your regret by saying, "I apologize." It's more positive because it is an act of doing rather than being.

Aquamarine Energy Strengthening Tips

Belt out a song in the shower. Hum along with music. Decorate your surroundings with turquoise, blue and pictures of the sea. Visit an aquarium. Have a pet gold fish. Put a fountain in a room where you can hear the water. Get a tape of the sound of rain. Go for a swim. Visit the ocean or put an ocean screensaver on your computer.

Affirmations

"I can express my truth easily. I hold nothing back."
"I deserve to make my feelings heard."
"My voice is clear and honest."
"I am comfortable expressing who I am."
"I release fear and doubts that block my creative expression."

PURPLE: Brow Chakra

Higher Intuition, Psychic Ability, Insight

"Intuition is when we know, but we don't know how we know."

~ Nancy Rosanoff

The Brow Chakra, also called the Third Eye, is located in the center of the forehead just above the physical eyes, right behind the brow bone. It is the center of your reality and your entire metaphysical universe: The Truth, The Spirit, The Light. As your "sixth sense," it helps you to view your path here on Earth. It is the center of discernment, wisdom, and intellectual thought.

"Fortunately, in order to navigate the terrain of our lives, we all come equipped with an inner guidance system which communicates with us through intuition or instinct, dreams, meetings, situations, 'chance' comments, synchronicities and health conditions. It works on the very simple basis that things feel right or they don't. However, for many of us our logic, our conditioning and societal and parental expectations override this still small voice within until we eventually learn to heed it come what may."
– Alison Adams at *www.thenaturalrecoveryplan.com*

The Balanced Brow Chakra

When your Brow Chakra is balanced, you have an ability to tune in to your Higher Self to receive inner guidance. Balanced purple energy allows us to see whether what we are doing is motivated by fear rather than an open connection. It supports our seeing the truth and not the illusion. It's no coincidence that purple grapes and wine fall into this color category. After all, *in vino veritas* – in wine there is truth.

The Underactive Brow Chakra

An underactive Brow Chakra can cause you to lose your feelings of being supported and your self-assertiveness. Without this inner guidance, you may feel lost, without a purpose or feel a part of you is missing.

The Overactive Brow Chakra

"A type of spiritual arrogance and ignorance can creep in when we over-value and over-indulge in 6th chakra pursuits. The result? We can become so heavenly minded we're no earthly good." –Janet Boyer

Did You Know...?

- The nutritional value of purple food is much higher than that of red food, black food or white food.
- Purple foods are loaded with powerful antioxidants called anthocyanins believed to protect against heart disease and may help delay the onset of Alzheimer's disease.
- The ability of anti-oxidation of anthocyanins is 30 to 50 times higher than that of vitamin C and that of vitamin E.
- Blueberries contain the largest number of anthocyanins among all the purple food. The anthocyanin present in blueberries is good for eye sight.
- According to the USDA, potatoes with the darkest colors have more than four times the antioxidant potential than other potatoes. Purple spuds score as high as Brussels sprouts, kale or spinach on the anti-oxidant power scale. These potatoes are also a good source of complex carbohydrates, potassium, vitamin C, folic acid and iron.
- Blueberries are one of the only natural foods that are blue in color.

Purple Foods

purple grapes • red wine • grape juice • prunes • blueberries • blackberries • black raspberries • eggplant • purple cabbage • purple onions • purple potatoes • purple cauliflower • blue corn • plums • raisins • purple peppers

PURPLE FOOD RECIPES

EGGPLANT STACKS

1 medium-size eggplant (about 1 pound, unpeeled, cut into rounds 1/2-inch thick)
2 small ripe tomatoes, cored and cut into 1/4-inch thick slices
1 tablespoon olive oil
1 tablespoon minced fresh basil or 1/2 teaspoon dried basil, crumbled
1/8 teaspoon fresh ground pepper
   Grated Parmesan cheese

1. Heat the oven to 375 degrees. Arrange the eggplant slices on a nonstick baking sheet and bake for 15 to 20 minutes or until the egg plant is fork-tender.
2. Increase the oven temperature to broil. Place a tomato slice on top of each eggplant round. Drizzle with olive oil over the tomatoes and sprinkle with the basil and pepper.
3. Place the baking sheet in the broiler, 5 to 6 inches from heat, and broil for 3 minutes or until the tomatoes are soft. Sprinkle with grated Parmesan cheese.

Yields 4 servings

BRAISED PURPLE CABBAGE WITH CRANBERRIES

1 tablespoon peanut oil or corn oil

1 medium onion, chopped

2 cloves garlic, minced

1 small head purple cabbage (about 1 pound), cored and sliced thin

1 cup cranberries

1 tablespoon red wine vinegar

1 tablespoon honey

   Juice of 1 orange (about 1/2 cup)

1 bay leaf

1 teaspoon finely grated ginger

1/8 teaspoon ground cloves

1. Heat the oil over medium heat in large skillet. Add the onion and garlic. Cook and stir until tender, about 5 minutes. Stir in the cabbage, cover and cook until the cabbage is barely wilted, about 10 minutes.

2. Add the cranberries, vinegar, honey, orange juice, bay leaf, ginger and cloves; cover, and continue cooking until almost all the liquid has evaporated and cabbage is completely wilted, about 10 minutes. If the cabbage has wilted but there is still considerable liquid left, remove the cover and raise the heat to high to boil down the liquid. Remove and discard the bay leaf.

Yields 4 servings

BLUEBERRY GREEN TEA SLUSHY

2 cups water
3 green tea bags
1 cup blueberries
1/2 cup water
2 tablespoons honey

1. Bring 2 cups of water to a boil. Add tea bags and let steep for 5 minutes. Remove tea bags.
2. Divide blueberries between the compartments of an ice cube tray. Cover with tea and freeze.
3. Purée in a blender with remaining tea, 1/2 cup water, and honey. Garnish with additional berries and mint.

Yields 4 servings

Let water cool at least 5 minutes before it goes in the ice cube trays.

OVEN-DRIED LEMON BLUEBERRIES

1 cup blueberries
1 teaspoon honey
1/2 teaspoon grated lemon rind

1. Heat oven to 225 degrees. Toss the blueberries with the honey and lemon rind in bowl.
2. Bake berries on a parchment-lined baking sheet until shriveled but still supple, about 2 hours. Let cool.
   Berries will keep in an airtight container for up to 1 month. Keep on hand to perk up salads, oatmeal, yogurt, and granola. Makes a great snack.

Yields 1 cup

ROASTED PURPLE ONIONS AND BRUSSELS SPROUTS

1 1/2 pounds brussels sprouts, trimmed and quartered

2 cloves garlic, thinly sliced

1 tablespoon olive oil

1 1/2 pounds purple onions, thickly sliced

1/4 cup balsamic vinegar

   Sea salt and pepper to taste

1. Heat the oven to 450 degrees. Line large baking sheet with nonstick foil.
2. Spread brussels sprouts and garlic in single layer on prepared pan and toss with oil. Roast in upper third of oven, stirring occasionally, 12 minutes.
3. Add onions to pan, tossing to combine, and continue roasting until vegetables are tender and lightly brown, about 10 minutes longer.
4. Drizzle with vinegar, tossing to combine and roast 2 minutes longer. Transfer to serving bowl and season to taste with sea salt and pepper.

Yields 6 to 8 servings

LAVENDER ICED TEA

4 quarts plus 1 cup water

1 1/2 cups honey or to taste

2 tablespoons dried culinary lavender buds*

12 tea bags

    Ice cubes

    Dried lavender sprigs (optional)

1. Bring 5 cups water, honey, and lavender to boil in large saucepan, stirring until honey dissolves. Boil until reduced to about 4 cups, about 14 minutes.
2. Bring remaining water to boil in large pot. Remove from heat. Add tea bags; steep 5 minutes. Strain into very large pitcher and let cool.
3. Fill 10 glasses with ice cubes. Pour about 1 cup over each glass. Stir in 4 to 6 tablespoons lavender syrup, adjusting to taste. Garnish with lavender, if desired.

Yields 10 servings

*Available at natural foods stores, at farmers markets, and by mail order.

Purple Exercises

Tapping Into Your Intuition

*"Imagination is everything.
It is the preview of life's coming attractions."*

~ Albert Einstein

Why would you want to increase your intuitive skills? Quite simply, it gives you more confidence in your hunches, allows you to better understand people and make more accurate decisions. It is your inner guidance, a quiet voice that you can hear when you are receptive to it.

Testing Your Intuition, Your Inner Compass

Everyone has a sixth sense, a gut feeling or an inner knowing. It is more available to some of us than others because our logical minds clutter the space of intuition. According to David Stevens, professional intuitive and founder of *Yoga of the Mind*, a meditation and intuition training service, *"Some see flashes of pictures, others have certain feelings, some just have pure knowingness."*

To build intuitive muscle, David Stevens, suggests his *Blind Reading*:

1. Sit down at a writing table with three blank index cards.
2. Think about a decision you are currently grappling with and write three solutions for it, one on each card.
3. Turn the cards blank-side-up, shuffle them and place them face-down on a table.
4. Run your hands over the cards and notice the feeling of each card.
5. Assign a percentage to each card based on how powerfully you're drawn to it.
6. Turn the cards over and take note of the answer with the highest percentage.

Guess Who Is Calling

Whenever the phone rings, guess who the caller is before you pick the phone up. You will be amazed by how often you will get it right. Track the success of your guesses and notice how quickly you make progress.

Predict Which Elevator Will Open First

This is a fun way to erase boredom waiting for the elevator, while it increases your skill at following hunches.

Did You Know...?

• Listening to classical music (Mozart and Beethoven, for example) can enhance the energies flowing to the Purple Chakra.

• Thirty minutes before you go to sleep at night and thirty minutes after you wake up, you are in an alpha state or hypnotic state. In this very relaxed state, you might imagine positive outcomes that you want to happen because they can more easily be directed to your subconscious mind.

Suggested Reading: Intuition Workout, A Practical Guide To Discovering And Developing Your Inner Knowing, by Nancy Rosanoff

Affirmations

"I allow my purple energy to flow so that I can trust my instincts."
"I open myself to my intuition and deepest knowing."
"I allow my positive inner vision to manifest."
"I trust whatever comes my way is for my highest good."
"I convert negative thoughts about myself and others to positive energy."
"I release whatever is blocking my path."

Violet: Crown Chakra

Connection To The Divine

*"Faith is taking the first step,
even when you don't see the whole staircase."*

- Dr. Martin Luther King, Jr.

Accessing Divine wisdom is unaffected by the foods we eat – it goes beyond the material and physical world to spirituality or a higher state of consciousness – a connection and understanding to the infinite, or universal power however you envision it. It is the deepest part of our being. The Crown Chakra is not considered in relation to our physical body. It is nourished by breathing and meditation that help enhance wisdom and spirituality.

The Balanced Crown Chakra

You can accept yourself as an integral part of the Universe, know your life's purpose, and feel a personal connection with the creative spirit in us all. With faith in a spiritual connection we have confidence, trust and acceptance. You are so in tune, you can achieve miracles in life. This gives our compass its North Star, so to speak. We can find our way, no matter what.

The Underactive Crown Chakra

When our Crown Chakra is closed, we can experience loneliness, confusion, depression and learning disabilities. When we are disconnected from our soul, we do not have the understanding of our own value and meaning of our life's purpose. This can result in chronic exhaustion, inability to make decisions and feeling isolated from the world.

"If this chakra doesn't function properly we experience this period as the 'dark night of the soul' as it was described in the poetry of St. John of the Cross. When we are distracted or overwhelmed by the difficulties and pain of life, we may experience loss of faith in a compassionate Divine force. We start to doubt our own belief that we are spiritual as issues of disbelief and depression cloud our inner knowing and overshadow our Divine nature...The greatest healer of this chakra when wounded is our ability to surrender to the Divine and to trust the spiritual process in our lives..."

– Willie Cloete at *oneyogalife.wordpress.com*

The Overactive Crown Chakra

When our Crown Chakra is out of balance, we are so immersed in spiritual matters we ignore the needs of our bodies. We can become spacey and in need of red energy to ground us. When the Crown Chakra is too open or spins too fast, mental health issues including manic depression can occur.

Halo or Chakra?

You may notice that in religious paintings there is a halo over the heads or surrounding the body of angels and saints. You also can see that the halo is either white, gold or violet. Some authors suggest that the Crown Chakra, the disk at the top of the head, is the same as the halos we see in religious renderings of angels and saints. The halo or Crown Chakra can be seen because of the highly spiritual connection between religious figures and the Universal Power.

Breathing And Meditation Exercises

All spiritual practice begins with quieting the mind, letting go of the daily chatter and rambling thoughts. To release regrets and to stop replaying old tapes, to get out of the shadow of darkness and fear, we need to go to an emotionally safe place in our minds. There are many, many guided imagery books and tapes available that show you how. Throughout this book, we are giving you a mini-sampling of them. The most powerful meditation of all is using your breath. In her book, *Chakra Foods For Optimum Health*, Deanna M. Minich says:

"We cannot assimilate the vibration of foods to feed our chakras unless we have the essential wiring in place to our Crown Chakra. With oxygen, our being stays conscious, alive and invigorated. Deep breathing and oxygenation therapies help to clear the Crown Chakra."

Let's Begin
(Do not do these exercises while driving a car, cooking or operating machinery)

First, select a quiet place where you won't be disturbed. The room should be at a comfortable temperature with the lights turned down low. You may choose to sit in a comfortable chair with your back, neck and arms sup-ported. Or lie down with a pillow under your knees and a cervical roll pillow or towel substitute under your neck. Your legs should be parallel and relaxed, not crossed. You may wish to take off your shoes and loosen any tight clothing.

The Basic Four Count Breath

- Breathe in slowly to a count of four.
- Hold the breath for a count of four.
- Exhale slowly through pursed lips to a count of four.
- Rest for a count of four without taking any breaths.
- Take two normal breaths.
- Start over again breathing in slowly to a count of four and repeat this exercise as many times as needed.

The Smiling Breath Meditation

One of our favorite simple breath visualizations is suggested by Dennis Lewis, founder of *The Center for Harmonious Awakening*. It begins with mindful appreciation of your life - this very second you are in it. No thoughts of the past, no thoughts of the future, just a smiling, shining moment.

"We have been given the miraculous gift of breath, of life. Pause for a moment and smile inwardly at this miracle. Breathe through your smile into your whole body, especially your heart. Let the warm light of your smiling awareness and breath touch and awaken every cell of your body until you feel a sense of silence and spaciousness."

– Dennis Lewis at *www.dennislewis.org*

Suggested Reading: "Breathe Deep, Laugh Loudly" by Dr. Judith Kravitz. To find out about her Transformational Breath Workshops, visit: http://www.transformationalbreathing.com

Affirmations

"My life has a purpose."
"I know that I am divinely guided."
"My knowing supports my faith."
"I am open to all the goodness there is."
"I am totally at peace with myself."
"I tune into my connection with the Divine."

"Life is more fun if you play games."

~ Roald Dahl, in the novel *My Uncle Oswald*

PART III

Playing With Rainbow Foods

Whether you are cooking to align your chakras or to enjoy a delicious beverage, soup, salad dressing or dish, you can maintain balanced emotional energy using a colorful recipe each day of the week. The important thing is for you to look at fruits and vegetables and know and appreciate their psychological and spiritual benefits as you eat them. That way, you are also sending positive balancing messages to your subconscious mind.

Remember, even if you are making a simple smoothie, it is good to mindfully acknowledge the benefit of each ingredient you put in. You might even add an affirmation or statement as you include ingredients. For example, when you put in a banana, which is yellow and resonates with a strong ego, confidence and intelligence, you might say to yourself, "I am strong, I am talented and I am confident. I have the intelligence to handle anything that comes my way."

THE RAINBOW BROTH
A Blend Of All Chakra Colors

Broths are the foundation for most cooking. It's the base for most soups, sauces, and stews. They are great when added to just about any ingredients for a flavor boost. Broth can also make a delicious sipping tea. They can provide a tremendous nutritional, emotional and spiritual boost anytime of the day. This Rainbow Broth contains ingredients and colors whose vibrations can activate or balance your emotional energies.

While our Rainbow Broth recipe is cleansing, healing and nourishing, we invite you to customize it to your particular needs. You simply select the color that corresponds to your emotional needs as you learned earlier, and select food or foods of the same color. The following recipe is great to use as an everyday broth. The Rainbow Broth is great to use as a salad dressing on a colorful Cobb Salad or as an ingredient in vegetable, chicken or bean soup.

THE RAINBOW BROTH RECIPE

2 large purple onions, sliced

1/4 small purple cabbage, sliced

4 celery ribs, sliced into 2-inch pieces

1/4 to 1/3 cup watercress

4 medium carrots, sliced into 2-inch pieces

1 medium parsnip, sliced into 1-inch pieces

The juice of one large lemon

2-inch piece ginger root, sliced

6 cloves garlic, sliced in half

1 1/2 gallons distilled or purified water

    Cayenne pepper to taste

    Sea salt to taste

1. Place ingredients in large stockpot, Dutch oven, or slow cooker.
2. Cover and simmer over very low heat (Do not boil) for 3 to 4 hours. Cook longer for more intense flavor if desired.
3. Skim if necessary. Strain, pressing down on vegetables to extract the juices. Let cool uncovered, then refrigerate covered.
4. Serve at room temperature.

Yields about 1 1/2 gallons

Customizing The Rainbow Broth Recipe To Add More Color

Let's say you wish to feel more love in your life. Perhaps you wish to heal old hurts or a recent loss. That corresponds to the Heart Chakra whose color is green. You would cook up your Rainbow Broth and add your choice of green foods to it. We invite you to experiment with the Rainbow Broth, adding ingredients to it to make it your own.

The Purée Shortcut For Individual Colors

Here's a quick and easy way for you to enjoy individual rainbow colors. You can create veggie purées in the blender and freeze them in muffin cups and bag them. That way, you can take them out of the freezer as needed and they become ingredients you can use in other recipes. You might start using them in soups, as gravies, salad dressings or in smoothies.

1. From the charts in PART I, select the color you need and use the corresponding vegetables.
2. Cut or slice the veggies. Blend until smooth.
3. Freeze the liquid in metal muffin cups about 1/3 cup each.
4. After the cups are frozen, empty the frozen broth cubes into an air tight container or freezer bags to keep handy in the freezer.

Try cooking fresh vegetables with the cubes or throw them in when you steam or poach fish or braise poultry and meats. It's great as a sipping tea with a little citric juice, ginger or a dash of nutmeg or cinnamon. It's great to throw into a smoothie too! The beauty of freezing the liquid in a muffin pan is that you can bag the cubes and take each cube out of the pan as needed. For example, melt them on veggies or add them to soups or sauces.

Vegetable Purée Tips

1. Remove fibrous parts, skins and seeds from vegetables.
2. Cut vegetables into small uniform pieces, so they cook at the same amount of time.
3. To make smoother purées, cook vegetables until done, without over-cooking them. Be careful with green vegetables, because overheating could happen and cause your green vegetables to turn that olive-gray color. Drain and let cool. Place a small amount of the cooled vegetables in blender or food processor and process until smooth. Repeat with remaining vegetables.
4. Watery vegetables like eggplant are better baked, roasted or stir-fried, rather than boiled. Boiling would cause watery vegetables to take on too much water.
5. The last step involves adding a little olive oil, broth, juice, or water for the desired consistency. This will give the purée richness and flavor.
6. To avoid ugly accidents, always allow the vegetables to cool slightly and only purée a small amount at a time. Hot foods can release a lot of steam when you purée them, blowing the top off your blender.

How To Throw A Rainbow Party

If you and your friends are into new things, why not host a *Rainbow Party*? You can build a party around tasting and learning about the color vibrations of food. A *Rainbow Party* is a great way to have fun and balance your emotions at the same time. In addition to the Rainbow Broth and purées, you can show your friends how to make the appetizers and *Rainbow Shooters*, and play The *Rainbow Party Card Game*. Here's how it works.

Invite six friends over and ask each to bring a different colored fruit or veggie dish. You suggest the color to each guest. Make sure you have all six colors, one per guest. You supply the white wine, red wine, Rainbow Broth, and puréed cooked vegetables (for each color).

COLORFUL PARTY APPETIZERS

MIXED BERRIES WITH FRESH ROSEMARY AND BISCOTTI

3 to 4 pints fresh berries (strawberries, blueberries, blackberries, raspberries)
2 tablespoons honey or agave
   Juice and grated zest of 1 lemon
1 tablespoon chopped fresh rosemary
1 package biscotti
   Rosemary Sprigs

1. Rinse the berries. Cut the strawberries in half lengthwise.
2. Gently combine the berries with honey, lemon juice and zest, and chopped rosemary, and let sit in refrigerator for at least 1 hour before serving.
3. To serve, spoon into bowls or compotes. Garnish with a sprig or two of fresh rosemary.

Yields about 8 servings

DILLY YOGURT DIP

1 16-ounce container plain Greek yogurt

1 medium cucumber, peeled, seeded and finely diced

2 cloves garlic, finely chopped

1/4 cup thinly sliced green onion or chives

2 teaspoons olive oil

2 teaspoons fresh lemon juice

1 tablespoon fresh dill weed or 1 teaspoon dried dill

1/2 teaspoon turmeric

1/2 teaspoon sea salt

   Dash cayenne

1. Line a mesh strainer with a paper coffee filter or paper towel. Spoon the yogurt into filter and place strainer over a bowl. Cover with plastic wrap and chill for 4 hours.
2. Spoon the yogurt into a bowl, discarding strained liquid. Stir in diced cucumber and remaining ingredients.
3. Cover and chill yogurt mixture until ready to serve. Garnish with dill if desired. Serve with a variety of colorful fresh vegetables.

Yields about 3 cups

HERBED OLIVES

3 cups mixed black and green brine-cured olives, such as Kalamata, picholine and Gaeta (about 3/4 pound)

3 tablespoons olive oil

1 to 1 1/2 tablespoons minced fresh thyme or 1 1/2 teaspoon dried thyme, crushed

1 teaspoon fresh grated lemon zest

2 cloves garlic, finely minced

1/2 teaspoon dried crushed red pepper or to taste

1. In a container with a tight-fitting lid combine all ingredients with sea salt and pepper to taste and chill in refrigerator.
2. Shake occasionally, store olives at least 1 day and up to 1 week.
3. Serve olives at room temperature.

Yields about 3 cups

RAINBOW SHOOTERS

Materials: 6 shot glasses, 6 spoons, 6 bowls - each to be filled with a different color purée

1. Let guests select whatever color they are working on.
2. Each guest places a desired color purée into their bowl and stirs in just enough *Rainbow Broth* to desired consistency.
3. Then each guest spoons their purée mixture into a shot glass. Every one can be creative and use different colors with the Rainbow Broth.

RAINBOW PARTY CARD GAME

Materials: plain white cards - seven per person, colored pens or pencils and *The Secret Powers Of Colorful Foods.*

You will be making a deck of seven cards for each guest, and handing out each deck, blank side up.

1. Place a different colored dot: red, orange, yellow, green, aquamarine purple, violet on each of seven cards, so that there's only one color per card. Make a deck of seven cards for each guest. Hand out the decks with dot side facing down.
2. Ask guests to close their eyes, and take several nice deep breaths. With their eyes closed, ask them to shuffle the cards, without turning any of the cards over. Still with eyes closed, have them select a card. Then, have them open their eyes and turn the selected card over. Each card's color represents a psychological or spiritual issue.
3. Each guest then writes down what the color represents to them on the card. If guests would like to share their issues and the colors related to them, the host or hostess of the party can read aloud from *The Secret Powers Of Colorful Foods* as a reference to review colors.

What's At The End Of Your Rainbow

There are many uses for what you have learned throughout this book. Whether it is you, a family member or a friend who seems to be dealing with an issue, you can help support well-being simply by serving a food whose color matches an attitude, outlook or emotion and by doing the exercises for each color.

Now that you know *The Secret Powers Of Colorful Foods*, you will notice a shift in the way you see rainbow foods. You may be surprised to find that you do not look at fruits and vegetables the way you used to.

We invite you to share your new knowledge with others, – whether it is sharing the book and the recipes and the exercises or playing with rainbow foods. It is good for the body, the psyche and the soul.

About The Authors

Patricia Dennis, M.S., C.Ht.

Educator, Writer, Hypnotherapist, Therapeutic Imagery Facilitator

An award-winning commercial writer and former associate creative director in advertising, she created print and broadcast for many accounts including Lawry's Foods, Nestle, Beatrice Hunt Wesson and Mondavi Wine at L.A. agencies Dailey and Associates and Benton and Bowles.

She holds a Master's Degree in Education and is an honors graduate of The Hypnosis Motivation Institute, a nationally accredited hypnosis training college and clinic of hypnotherapy in Tarzana, California. HMI has earned the distinction of being America's first hypnotherapy training school to become nationally accredited by an accrediting agency recognized by the U.S. Department of Education, in Washington, D.C.

In addition to being a certified hypnotherapist and Therapeutic Imagery Facilitator she is a Past Life Therapist certified by Past Life pioneer, Dr. Morris Netherton. She uses her counseling techniques to offer a fresh approach to appreciating the energetic effects of nourishment.

Charlotte Lyons, B.S.

Magazine Food Editor, Cookbook Author, Educator, Culinary Consultant

Charlotte Lyons is an independent culinary consultant and the former food editor of *EBONY*, the world's number one African-American magazine. She served in this role beginning in 1985 and has more than thirty years experience in food preparation and guest entertainment. In 1999, she authored *The New EBONY Cookbook*. Charlotte has developed a loyal fan base and receives numerous requests to appear on entertainment news programs, cooking segments, and at community events.

She is a graduate of Morris Brown College in Atlanta, with a B.S. degree in Home Economics and Education. Her interest in cooking developed in early childhood in the kitchens of both her mother and grandmother. Prior to joining *EBONY* magazine, Charlotte mastered her skills in recipe development, food styling and new product development in several companies including The Betty Crocker Test Kitchen at General Mills and the Campbell Soup Company.

Today, Charlotte enjoys creating new recipes and adding a personal touch to traditional recipes. She is a sought after speaker and event planner, and demonstrates ways to prepare healthy meals for seniors, children, schools, churches and health organizations including The National Kidney Foundation.

BIBLIOGRAPHY

Batmanghelidj, F.
   Your Body's Many Cries For Water. Tagman Press. 2004.

Bradford, Michael
   The Healing Energy of Your Hands. Crossing Press. 1993.

Caponigro, Andy
   The Miracle Of The Breath: mastering fear, healing illness, and experiencing the Divine. New World Library. 2005.

Dale, Cyndi
   The Complete Book Of Chakra Healing: activate the transformative power of your energy centers. Llewellyn Publications. 2010.

Dincalci, Jim
   How To Forgive When You Can't: the breakthrough guide to free your heart and mind: healing upsets without condoning or being hurt again. The Forgiveness Foundation. 2010.

Gardner, Joy
   Vibrational Healing Through The Chakras. Crossing Press. 2006.

Gawain, Shakti
   Creative Visualization. New World Library. 1995.

Hay, Louise L.
   Heart Thoughts, A Treasury of Inner Wisdom. Hay House. 1990.
   You Can Heal Your Life. Hay House. 1990.
   Love Yourself, Heal Your Life Workbook. Hay House. 1990.

Judith, Anodea
   Eastern Body, Western Mind: Psychology and the chakra system as a path to the self. Celestial Arts. 2004.

Minich, Deanna M.
   Chakra Foods For Optimum Health: a guide to the foods that can improve your energy, inspire creative changes, open your heart, and heal body, mind, and spirit. Conari Press. 2009.

Naparstek, Belleruth
    Staying Well With Guided Imagery: how to harness the power of your imagination for health and healing. Warner Books. 1994.

O'Neil, Cheryl
    Therapeutic Imagery: Professional Training and Certification Program. Pathfinder. 2001.

Pert, Candace
    Molecules of Emotion. Simon and Schuster, Inc. 1991.

Rosanoff, Nancy
    Intuition Workout: a practical guide to discovering and developing your inner knowing. Aslan Publishing. 1991.

Rossman, Martin, L.
    Guided Imagery for Self-Healing. New World Library. 2000.

Shaw, Paula
    Chakras: The Magnificent Seven Energy Centers For Healing. After Midnight Press. 2002.

Singer, Michael
    The Untethered Soul: the journey beyond yourself. New Harbinger Publications and Noetic Books. 2007.

Truman, Karol K.
    Feelings Buried Alive Never Die. Olympus Distributing. 1991.

Wauters, Ambika
    Homeopathic Color And Sound Remedies. Crossing Press. 2001.

Wells, Valerie
    The Joy Of Visualization: 75 creative ways to enhance your life. Chronicle Books. 1990.

ONLINE ARTICLES

squidoo.com/spectralpalate#module152491564

befityoga.com/philosophy-lifestyle/chakras/

theresurrectionofhumptydumpty.com/2011/07/how-healthy-is-your-first-chakra/

blog.deanramsden.com/chakra-cords-extend-the-mind/

crystalinks.com

threeheartscompany.com/chakra.html

myenergyhealing.net/chakras.htm

divavillage.com/article/id/47072/section name/Empower

muse-net.com/chakramed-html/

alternativeculture.com/spirit/chakras.htm

janetboyer.com